# EMPOWERING YOUR HUMAN SPIRIT AND MENTAL HEALTH

*by*
*Dr. Shon Shree Lewis*

# TABLE OF CONTENTS

Book Introduction                                                      v
About the Author                                                       vii

Chapter 1    The Human Spirit                                          1
Chapter 2    The Brain's Development                                   5
Chapter 3    Your Thought Life                                         7
Chapter 4    Crisis & Trauma                                           15
Chapter 5    Dealing with Church Hurt                                  29
Chapter 6    Movie Case Study                                          43
Chapter 7    Understanding the Dream and Vision Realm                  49
Chapter 8    Sobriety                                                  67
Chapter 9    The Power of Fasting                                      73
Chapter 10   The Secret Power of Foods                                 77
Chapter 11   The Power of Imagination                                  81
Chapter 12   The Power of Meditation                                   87
Chapter 13   The Power of Words                                        99
Chapter 14   The Power of Music                                        103
Chapter 15   The Power of Wisdom                                       107
Chapter 16   Reshaping the Soul                                        111
Chapter 17   Spiritual Care and More                                   123

Mental Health Checkup                                                  131
References                                                             133

# BOOK INTRODUCTION

Salvation and knowledge are *gifts from God* to you. His Word is life-giving for any area of life. Therefore my book will discuss biblical truths, spiritual knowledge, and psychological theories and truths, identifying and revealing how human development, parental styles, environment, spiritual beings, and physical health can make or break your mental health and spiritual wellness. Learning the power of imagination and meditation will give each reader life-changing insight, knowledge, mental health methods, and spiritual principles to transform and empower your whole being. Each page of my book will also empower you to integrate biblical truths, spiritual knowledge, psychology, and medical wisdom into living a well-balanced life holistically.

As a *disclaimer*, remember that biblical, spiritual, and psychological knowledge is progressive. New revelations that are more enlightening can be discovered through time as you empower yourself with information and credible research for your health and wellness. Developing a personal relationship with God will help guide you to all truths in life.

So, your *human experience* in life is to be enlightening, adventurous, and rewarding to you holistically. As a result, you will holistically embrace your *human experience*, enjoy your spiritual, mental, and physical health, value yourself, be free from mental illnesses, and live your best life!

# ABOUT THE AUTHOR

Dr. Shon Shree Lewis is an Apostle, Prophetess, and Doctor of Divinity Ph.D, Doctor of Theology, Mental Health Counselor, Certified Professional Life Coach, Author, and Entrepreneur of Inspirational products from Milwaukee, Wisconsin.

In **1995,** Dr. Shon Shree Lewis gave her life to God, accepting Jesus as her Lord and Savior and receiving his Holy Spirit.

**2003** Dr. Shon Shree Lewis earned her Associate degree in Theology, contributing to her spiritual education and her born gift of writing.

**2013**, She earned her paralegal degree at Bryant & Stratton College in Wauwatosa, Wisconsin.

**2015**, Dr. Shon Shree Lewis published her first book "Overcoming The Seesaw of Wisdom Against Fear," which began to bless and help many hearts worldwide, heal from fear of evil and life's challenges by learning how to receive and use God's power.

**2017**, Dr. Shon Shree Lewis received an Honorary Doctorate Theology degree from GMOR Theological Institute of America in Munster, Indiana.

**2018,** Dr. Shon Shree Lewis published one of her popular books,

"The Weapons Of The Mind," is now worldwide in colleges and libraries used widely in other countries for theological and mental health studies.

In **2019**, she became a licensed Christian Pastor.

By **January 2020**, she earned her Doctor of Divinity Ph.D. Degree from Grace Christian College from Loris, South Carolina.

Shortly after she earned her Doctor of Divinity Ph.D., she also began to pursue her Bachelor of Behavioral Science at Liberty University College for Interdisciplinary Studies, with specialties in: crisis trauma, psychology, and government studies.

**December 2021**, Dr. Shon Lewis earned her Bachelor of Behavioral Science in Interdisciplinary Studies at Liberty University College, including specialty studies to help counsel others to heal from crisis & trauma, spiritually and professionally, toward a life of resilience and lasting eternal power in God.

In **2021**, Dr. Shon Lewis published another powerful Mental Health book titled, "Untraumatized," available where books are sold, a mental health guide, and her memoir for healing the mind, soul, and spirit of humanity from a psychological and spiritual perspective. This book is available as a hardcover, paperback, audiobook, ebook, along with some of her other faith-based inspirational books.

She also began her popular children's book Coco's Life Adventures, some available where books are sold. By 2023, she also published a new children's book titled "Andy Can: Be Different," beginning a new series of The Chronicles of Andy future additional books. These books provide children with learning skills for a healthy self-image, morals, and values for developing healthy family relationships, creativity, and educational and social skills.

**March 2023**, Dr. Shon Lewis earned her Master's Degree in Human Services Counseling: Crisis & Response Trauma at Liberty University College. She has facilitated support groups for substance abuse and recovery and Divorce care support groups and continues this life work to promote healing in people's lives. She continues empowering people worldwide to live for Jesus and a life of healing, purpose, stability, and joy.

# CHAPTER 1

# THE HUMAN SPIRIT

Suppose you are a spiritual person and a person of faith, believing in the supernatural invisible power of God. In that case, you will understand that your *human spirit* didn't just exist by happenstance. God, the invisible deity, created all living things, including the heavens and humanity, created your human spirit. As you know, this process usually happens during conception of a baby. God plants the human spirit into a woman's womb, and the baby grows into a physical body and later is born. But not just born with a spirit within in the body; the body also carries a *soul*. The soul will be explained in a later chapter. Some people think having biblical knowledge is the same as being spiritual, but it is not. A person can have biblical knowledge and memorize it but not have a connection with God, which is spiritual. Therefore, to understand how to manage your mental health and develop spiritual wellness, especially when healing and recovery are needed from life crises and distress, you must be a spiritual person and understand the spiritual world first.

Your human spirit came from God. Let's see what the Bible says about it. Genesis 1:26-27 (KJV) says,

And God said, Let us make man in our image, after our likeness: and let them have dominion over the fish of the sea, and over the fowl of the air, and over the cattle, and over all the earth, and over every creeping thing that creepeth upon the earth. So God created man in his own image, in the image of God created he him; male and female created he them. Here is the Genesis of how humanity was created.

Furthermore, Genesis 2:7 (KJV) says, "And the Lord God formed man of the dust of the ground, and breathed into his nostrils the breath of life; and man became a living soul." Notice this passage says God breathed (life) into humanity, and he (Adam) became a *living soul.* The soul is the brain (mind), will (desires), and emotions (feelings) of a human being. So your human spirit lives in your body, which carries your soul (your mind, will, and emotions).

## Wounded Spirits

Did you know that your human spirit is in your belly? Proverbs 20:27 (KJV) says, "The spirit of a man is the candle of the Lord, searching all the inward parts of the belly." Here the scripture is letting you know where God placed your human spirit and how He examines it, whether it be evil or holy. Moreover, think about when you feel intuition. Some people say from their gut. Others feel anger in the pit of their belly. This energy is where their human spirit feels the weight of emotions of their soul.

The human spirit can be wounded or broken. A person's spirit becomes damaged by abusive and hurtful people. Proverbs 26:22 (KJV) states, "The words of a talebearer are as wounds, and they go down into the innermost parts of the belly." Notably, the scripture references evil words spoken to someone can deeply wound a person's spirit. This can happen in families, friendships, and people in the church speaking negative words, rejection, or mistreatment. Proverbs 18:14 (KJV) says, "The spirit of a man will sustain his infirmity; but a wounded spirit who can bear?" Proverbs 18:14 (AMPC) says, "The strong spirit of a man sustains him in bodily pain or trouble, but a weak and broken spirit who can raise up or bear?" The International Children's Bible (ICB) translation says, "The will to live can get you through sickness. But no one can live with a broken spirit."

Comparatively, Proverbs 12:25 (KJV) says, "Heaviness in the heart of a man maketh it stoop: but a good word maketh it glad." Notably, a person's heart can be one's human spirit intertwined with one's soul. So when a person feels hopeless because of hurtful people or adversities they have experienced in their lives, a kind word or encouragement about their value as a person from someone can lift a person's spirit. However, God is the healer. His Word, communion with Him through prayer, and support from other saints of God provide the healing path for the wounded. God's Word will lift your spirit.

From generation to generation, through centuries and eras, humanity has populated and grown into families and nations, facing many adversities and challenges. However, God created each individual to live unto Him, in purity, with great purpose, to live a life of peace of blessings to help others. Once you understand the foundation and purpose of how and why the human spirit was created and formed, and your purpose from God, this is essential to understanding how to deal with your mental health and spiritual wellness. Since life has a way of interfering with the purpose of God, you need to be spiritually and mentally equipped on how to stay connected to God through growing in a relationship with Him while understanding the science of your mind, your cognitive abilities, and physical health, and how to integrate these critical factors holistically into your mental health and spiritual wellness as a lifestyle.

# CHAPTER 2
# THE BRAIN'S DEVELOPMENT

You must know what you are made of and how that governs your mental and physical health. Along with your spirit, your brain is vital to your human functioning. The brain influences thought processes, personality, and behaviors. This process begins with a woman when she carries her child during pregnancy. A woman's mental state and physical health influence how healthy her baby develops before birth. Notably, it is essential an expectant mother, avoid hostile people and places.

One of these processes is called *neuroplasticity*. Different research explains neuroplasticity as the forming of the brain, involving the communication of nerve impulses that helps a person learn and comprehend things to function. Notably, if a pregnant mother is suffering from distress, or trauma, her human spirit, psychological state, and physical condition will affect an unborn child. On the other hand, a healthy mother, mentally and physically, will have greater chance of carrying a healthy child. However, those who struggle with mental health issues, drugs, alcoholism, and depression, can pass these traits to their children through their genes and bloodline. The father's genetics can also affect a child's mental health; if there were mental illnesses such as schizophrenia or depression, the father suffered for a time. Just like diseases, such as diabetes, can pass genetically from a child to a parent, mental health issues and addictions can also be passed on to children.

Furthermore, recent research shows the prenatal stages appear to contribute to the development of one's brain, which can either positively or negatively affect how it is structured and functions as one age into adulthood.

So keep in mind the healthiness of the brain process continues throughout a person's human development as a person grows into adolescence and adulthood. As a result, the condition of the brain and how it functions will affect how the human mind develops and different thought patterns that can govern a person's life. That is why expectant mothers of birthing children must be spiritually, physically, and mentally well. Because if they are not, their children can be born with biological issues and mental impairment.

# CHAPTER 3

# YOUR THOUGHT LIFE

Are you *conscious* of your thoughts, and do you know the condition of your *conscience*? It is essential that you know the distinction between your *conscience* and being *conscious*. As you know, your thoughts make up your conscience, forming thoughts inside your mind. Notably, your thoughts are ideas and images from specific influences in this world that impact your interpretation and perception of people, places, and things. What a person stores in their mind through information, knowledge, television, listening to others, and images governs their mental health positively or negatively. That is why it is essential to analyze a thought by the sound, interpretation, and feeling it brings to you and ask yourself, what emotion do you experience and how does it influence and affect your actions?

Realize that you were created from the spiritual world by God. If you are a spiritual person or a person of faith, it will be easy for you to understand thoughts are spiritual, to your mind from a invisible demonic spirit or from God, the Creator of humanity and the entire world. Realize because your thoughts are spiritual, they can open portals to the spiritual world and encounters with God and other spiritual beings. Knowing where your thoughts are coming from and how to filter and manage them is essential to your mental health and spiritual wellness.

## The Power of the Pineal Gland

Are you aware of the pineal gland in your brain and how it impacts your thought life and spiritual senses? Various biological

7

and psychological studies show how this gland in the forehead of the brain controls the spiritual connection into the spiritual world, for example, the (dream realm), to tap into supernatural insight from God to spiritual knowledge and happenings in the spirit world that can affect someone's waking life. Its purpose is not to engage with demonic powers to hurt others or defy God. On the contrary, remembering we were designed by God, including the pineal gland, is one of the ways to connect with Him and receive His guidance. Notably, some religious people and Christians debate the concept of any human being having a third eye. Some embrace it because of the biological explanation of the pineal gland and how it affects humanity's ability to process thoughts and connect with the spiritual world as God intended. Others have demonized the term (third eye) as a form of evil or engaging in wickedness. But this is not true. Whether people call the pineal gland the third eye or not, the pineal gland is not only designed by God for mental health but also for spiritual connection to Him.

There is an example in scripture, if you look at Genesis 32:24-30 (KJV) says,

> And Jacob was left alone; and there wrestled a man with him until the breaking of day. And when he saw that he prevailed not against him, he touched the hollow of his thigh; and the hollow of Jacob's thigh was out of joint, as he wrestled with him. And he said, Let me go, for the day breaketh. And he said, I will not let thee go, except thou bless me. And he said unto him, What is thy name? And he said, Jacob. And he said, Thy name shall be called no more Jacob, but Israel; for as a prince hast thou power with God and with men, and hast prevailed. And Jacob asked him, and said, Tell me, I pray thee, thy name. And he said, Wherefore is it that thou dost ask after my name? And he blessed him there. And Jacob called the name of the place *Peniel:* for I have seen God face to face, and my life is preserved.

Wow! Look at this experience Jacob (Israel) had with God, physically and supernaturally. Do you see how Jacob named the place

Peniel? Which means face-to-face or spiritual connection with God? Look at the correlation of the place called Peniel and the pineal gland in the human brain which allows for spiritual sensory of the spirit world and to connect with God. So there is a *mystery* about how God created the pineal gland for His glory for humanity to have consciousness and knowledge of the spirit world, for His purposes, not for evil.

Another example is the story of Elisha and his servant, who were facing a battle with an enemy from 2 Kings 6:15-17 (KJV) which says,

> And when the servant of the man of God was risen early, and gone forth, behold, an host compassed the city both with horses and chariots. And his servant said unto him, Alas, my master! how shall we do? And he answered, Fear not: for they that be with us are more than they that be with them. And Elisha prayed, and said, Lord, I pray thee, open his eyes, that he may see. And the Lord opened the eyes of the young man; and he saw: and, behold, the mountain was full of horses and chariots of fire round about Elisha.

Here, Elisha, the young man with him, and their army were being pursued by an evil army for battle. But Elisha was calm and trusted God. However, the young man that was with him did not. So after Elisha prayed to God for Him to open (the young man's spiritual eye), the young man could see into the spiritual world of the angelic beings and protection of God that surrounded Elisha and him. The pineal gland was also be in operation for the young man to see into the spiritual realm.

Another example in the Bible is the story about the woman Jesus found at the well. Although she was there to fetch water, Jesus had spiritual insight from God about her history of failed relationships in marriages. To illustrate, John 4:13-19 (KJV) says,

> Jesus answered and said unto her, Whosoever drinketh of this water shall thirst again: But whosoever drinketh of the water that I shall give him shall never thirst; but the water that I shall give him shall be in him a well of water springing

up into everlasting life. The woman saith unto him, Sir, give me this water, that I thirst not, neither come hither to draw. Jesus saith unto her, Go, call thy husband, and come hither. The woman answered and said, I have no husband. Jesus said unto her, Thou hast well said, I have no husband: For thou hast had five husbands; and he whom thou now hast is not thy husband: in that saidst thou truly. The woman saith unto him, Sir, I perceive that thou art a prophet.

Notice how Jesus had spiritual knowledge of this stranger woman's life? How could Jesus have known about her life without God empowering him with this knowledge through his spiritual eye? The woman at the well also acknowledged him as a prophet, knowing he could see into her past through supernatural power from God. See how our brain works with the spiritual realm?

Sadly, wicked people can corrupt what God created for good to use for wicked purposes, but God's creation is still pure. That is why it is critical people must learn to integrate spirituality from God with science and how God designed the human anatomy to function for His glory. More will be explained later in the dream chapter.

Your human spirit and thoughts are also influenced by the physical world. Namely, they are people, places, and things that cause personal experiences. For example, starting in early childhood, children are easily influenced by their parent's or guardians' beliefs, lifestyles, behaviors, and environments, whether positive or negative. In early and middle childhood, how parents interact with their children and the structure of their home life can impact their children's thought processes and how their persona develops and transforms. The Bible also says from Proverbs 23:7 (KJV), "For as he thinketh in his heart, so is he: Eat and drink, saith he to thee; but his heart is not with thee." In other words, how a child, adolescent, or adult perceives themselves will influence how they treat themselves and others. Notably, your self-concept or self-image will affect how you feel about yourself and relate with others. This is why it is critical for children must be raised and taught by loving parents and guardians in a safe and caring home. Self-image is vital to a child's personal growth and mental health as they emerge into adolescence into their adulthood.

Another influence of one's thoughts is demonic spirits from the spiritual world. For those who are not spiritual or struggle with believing in God, it will be difficult to understand how this works. Understand life is lived by an invisible power called *faith.* Suppose a person doesn't believe in the truth about spirituality. In that case, it will be difficult for this person to receive the help and the healing needed to overcome psychological disturbances and mental illnesses. One way to recognize a demonic spirit bringing a negative thought to you is to analyze if the thought is against God. Another way is to examine if the idea brings negative feelings of sadness, depression, low self-esteem, and suicide against you. Also, recognizing a thought about hurting someone or destroying someone is a sign of a demonic presence attacking your mind. This is dangerous to your mental health and others if you don't understand how to resist and counterattack these thoughts. To illustrate, at the beginning of time on the earth, when God created the first man Adam and the first woman Eve, they lived in paradise in the garden of Eden among many beautiful trees with fruit. Adam, however, was instructed directly by God not to eat of the tree of the knowledge of good and evil because, as a result, it would cause spiritual death and separation from God. Genesis 3:1-8, (KJV) says,

> Now the serpent was more subtil than any beast of the field which the Lord God had made. And he said unto the woman, Yea, hath God said, Ye shall not eat of every tree of the garden? And the woman said unto the serpent, We may eat of the fruit of the trees of the garden: But of the fruit of the tree which is in the midst of the garden, God hath said, Ye shall not eat of it, neither shall ye touch it, lest ye die. And the serpent said unto the woman, Ye shall not surely die: For God doth know that in the day ye eat thereof, then your eyes shall be opened, and ye shall be as

gods, knowing good and evil. And when the woman saw that the tree was good for food, and that it was pleasant to the eyes, and a tree to be desired to make one wise, she took of the fruit thereof, and did eat, and gave also unto her husband with her; and he did eat. And the eyes of them were both opened, and they knew that they were naked; and they sewed fig leaves together, and made themselves aprons. And they heard the voice of the Lord God walking in the garden in the cool of the day: and Adam and his wife hid themselves from the presence of the Lord God amongst the trees of the garden.

Here is an example of how the invisible spirit, Satan or the devil, used the body of a snake to talk to Eve, making suggestions to Eve in her thoughts to disobey God, twisting God's words. As a result, the fall of humanity happened many centuries ago, which caused curses and wickedness to spread throughout the earth. Adam and Eve's choice to disobey God cost them their eviction from the Garden of Eden and gave the devil temporary power on the earth to influence evil behaviors in humanity.

On the other hand, those of you who are spiritual and believe God to be your Creator are in a position of empowerment about your spiritual and mental health. Once you understand that many centuries and decades later, after Adam and Eve's fall, Jesus Christ was sent later to redeem humanity from curses and sin to a life of purity unto God. Jesus later empowered humanity to resist the devil and demonic powers through his love, power, and purity from sin and his blood he shed on the cross to cleanse all humankind from sin.

So now, it is a choice for each individual to choose to live for God or the devil. But Jesus empowers those who accept him into their hearts, through repentance of sin to resist evil and overcome it. Romans 10:9 (KJV) explains from apostle Paul, saying, "That if thou shalt confess with thy mouth the Lord Jesus, and shalt believe in thine heart that God hath raised him from the dead, thou shalt be saved." This is one of the best life-changing decisions you can ever make, to live for God and learn how to live in the spiritual and physical realms of God. So, your words of confession, accepting Jesus into your heart, begin your redemption from darkness and destruction and begins inner healing in your life. Following this significant decision, a person can pray and receive the Holy Spirit, Who continues to empower them to live a pure life and build a healthy relationship with God.

What is more, Romans 12th Chapter (KJV) talks about changing one's thinking patterns and thought processes. Romans 12:1-2 (KJV) says,

> I beseech you therefore, brethren, by the mercies of God, that ye present your bodies a living sacrifice, holy, acceptable unto God, which is your reasonable service. And be not conformed to this world: but be ye transformed by the renewing of your mind, that ye may prove what is that good, and acceptable, and perfect, will of God.

So, reading and studying the holy scriptures of God's mind for how you should live cleanses and renews your mind and your thought patterns and leads you to paths of purpose, joy, and blessings. 2 Corinthians 10:4-5 (AMP) says,

> The weapons of our warfare are not physical [weapons of flesh and blood]. Our weapons are divinely powerful for the destruction of fortresses. We are destroying sophisticated arguments and every exalted and proud thing that sets itself up against the [true] knowledge of God, and we are taking every thought and purpose captive to the obedience of Christ.

Again, God's Word, read and spoken, changes your thought processes from your human thinking to His way of thinking and how to live. Proverbs even talk about how committing your ways to God will establish your thoughts. Proverbs 16:3 (KJV) says, "Commit thy works unto the Lord, and thy thoughts shall be established." This simply means choosing to seek God by making a spiritual connection with Him, with a desire to live a moral and holy life, pure unto God, which will cause God to give you new ideas and paths leading to divine connections with others and blessings. Remember,

God will not bring you evil thoughts to make you feel bad about yourself.

On the contrary, God loves you. He will speak words of love, comfort, and correction to you. God will give you ideas of clarity for guidance and peace to answer questions for your life. Jeremiah 29:11 (AMP) says, "For I know the plans and thoughts that I have for you,' says the Lord, 'plans for peace *and* well-being and not for disaster, to give you a future and a hope." He shows you through His Word and by talking to your human spirit, words of truth and guidance to bring healing and wholeness to you that will transform your life for the better.

# CHAPTER 4

## CRISIS & TRAUMA

Going through a devastating event in your life is a painful experience. It can alter your life. However, realize your life is not over. There is hope for healing and recovery for you.

Therefore, when looking at crisis and trauma, you must understand how to identify what they are to *assess* if you have been through this experience. These tragedies can happen involuntarily or voluntarily. Understanding these experiences is necessary for you to get the help needed for your healing and recovery. This is vital for the condition of your mental health and spiritual well-being.

Did you know there is a difference between a *crisis* and *trauma?* A *crisis* is an event that causes someone *shock, fear, numbness, anger, sadness, confusion, vulnerability, stress*, and *self-pity* that has happened randomly in someone's life but can have lasting, devastating effects, causing mental disorders and a lack of human functioning. Furthermore, did you know that your soul is in your human spirit? Your soul is your *mind, will*, and *emotions*. Notably, when a person has experienced tragedies that have altered their livelihood and mental health, their *soul can become sick*, causing mental weakness and mental impairment, making it difficult for them to control their emotions and function as usual. Based on research, after you or someone you know experiences a crisis, if the person continues to suffer from lingering symptoms of anxiety, denial, fear, depression, sadness, or anger for more than three weeks, this person is now suffering from *trauma*. Trauma is the results from a crisis, which negatively impacts a person's mental health and human functioning, which can have lasting, devastating effects. Trauma produces symptoms of emotional problems from the crisis a person experiences.

Complex Trauma is a more severe level of trauma. A person who continues to experience repeated crises without professional treatment is experiencing complex trauma. As a result, complex trauma causes side effects such as fear, insomnia, emotional problems, *post-traumatic stress disorder* and mental disorders, dysfunctional behaviors, relational problems with others, and issues in social settings.

Notably, a crisis survivor does not need to be strong after a crisis. This person simply needs strength for each day. That is why it is critical to get professional help when this happens. Professional counseling is vital for the healing and recovery process to begin.

## Domestic Violence

There are common types of crises and trauma. One of them is toxic relationships. In a family home, some spouses experience intimate partner relationship violence and *verbal abuse*. Sadly, the abused spouse and their children are mentally scarred and mentally damaged.

***Effects.*** Consequently, there are physical wounds on domestic violence survivors that can be painful physically but also distort their appearance. These severe physical effects need medical attention for the survivors' physical healing. Domestic violence survivors, whether male or female, will struggle with decision-making for themselves, human functioning, and relational issues with others. Emotionally, many victims feel worthless, feel self-blame, angry, disappointed, and scarred from the abuse inflicted by their abuser. Notably, women of domestic violence suffer physical and mental turmoil and safety issues. There are also lasting psychological and emotional effects for youth experiencing the trauma of domestic violence. The emotional damage domestic violence causes a child or teen will result in certain disturbances in their behaviors toward others.

## Sexual Abuse

A different type of abuse is sexual violations. Sexual violence of unwanted sexual touch, activity, and abuse from another person, whether molestation or rape, is immoral and devastating for a victim to go through at any age. The effects on a person's soul and body can be devastating.

*Effects.* There are traumatic physical effects on someone who has been sexually assaulted. Because sexual violence can include unwanted aggression and resistance from the victim because of the abuser, the survivors can experience physical scars, bruises, and pain from the assault. There are also psychological effects on survivors of sexual violence. Other victims may feel petrified, disoriented, and dirty, so they disassociate themselves from processing the tormenting feelings of the sexual violation with the possibility of pregnancy or disease, resorting to memory lapse of the details of the abuse leading to mental dysfunction.

## Intimate Partner Violence (IPV)

Similarly, Intimate Partner Violence (IPV) is common in relationships, whether in marriage or romantic partnerships. In many cases, because the abuser lives in the home with the victim, the abuse is ignored, or the victims fear vengeance from the abuser to bring more harm to them after separation or are afraid of losing access to their necessities. Others become numb to the abuse and accept it with no planned resolution.

*Responses.* Survivors of sexual violations can react negatively to how they function in life due to the trauma they suffered. The rejection of not being believed can cause confusion and delusions of why the assault happened, frustration, and psychological distress to victims. Also, when a sexual assault victim is ignored by family or law enforcement, their sense of safety can push victims to feelings of depression, despair, and suicidal thoughts.

# Divorce Impact on Children

Divorce's impact on children is considered a devastating event and a critical time in children's human development because of the constant cognitive and physical changes children experience during the early stages of their development. The tearing of the family unit affects a child's psychological state, emotional well-being, and spiritual condition. Divorce is also a dramatic change to children's sense of safety and livelihood, and can impact their development.

Children experiencing their parents split up is a life-altering event during the development of their lives. This occurrence automatically interrupts stability in their lives, causing a drastic change in their livelihood. Notably, there are three areas of their lives where young people experience dramatic changes which impact their human development psychologically, emotionally, and spiritually.

*Effects.* First, children's identity is shaken when their parents tragically lose control over their relationship, with whom children have always known to be their rock, role model, and foundation of living. Here, a good relationship between their parents was not modeled to them, so they have no point of reference from their home life. Therefore, these children will have relational issues with others in future relationships. Children will struggle with their self-esteem and self-worth because seeing their parents fail in a relationship will distort their perception of conflict resolution. Notably, because children's identity is connected to their parents, hearing derogatory comments about a parent they admire or feel close to can tarnish how they see themselves.

# Personal Growth and Recovery

Differently, children going through the parental divorce process experience personal growth while navigating and adjusting to their parent's split. Some parents need professional and family counseling to recover from a divorce crisis. When parents get the professional help they need and work through their differences legally in a civil way, their children can adjust to the divorce of the parents much easier. This helps children cognitively and emotionally to bear through adversities with the inner strength to recover from them.

## Covid19

Covid-19, one of the most deadly international pandemics, has caused masses of people to suddenly and quickly become gravely ill or slip away to death. Many people developed fear from the dread of catching the disease and losing so many loved ones worldwide rapidly. When masks were required with social distancing, it heightened some people's anxiety temporarily, while others felt some comfort but still not at ease. Others took vaccination shots. This is a personal decision and should not be forced on anyone.

However, during worldwide pandemics, there are solutions to prevent distress and post-traumatic stress for peace of mind. First, simply use good hygiene, including keeping your hands clean with soap and water as necessary, is essential for your safety and mental health. Be cautious of people who cough and sneeze in their hands. If you see this, do not shake their hands or hug them unless you know they have thoroughly washed their hands with soap and water. If someone around you has a cold or signs of Covid19 or any airborne disease, social distancing and recommending getting tested would be the wise thing to do. On the other hand, if you are the one with cold symptoms, get tested and use social distancing to prevent the spread of germs, even if you don't have Covid19. It's good to be sure about your health to prevent of any airborne disease and sickness. What is equally important is staying prayerful. Praying for God's protection and safety is always powerful. Psalm 91:5-7 (NIV) says,

> You will not fear the terror of night, nor the arrow that flies by day, nor the pestilence that stalks in the darkness, nor the plague that destroys at midday. A thousand may fall at

your side, ten thousand at your right hand, but it will not come near you.
Meditate this Word from God and pray it, and it will sustain you.

## Natural Disasters

There are severe mental health issues survivors of disasters experience after encountering dramatic witnessing of disturbing scenes and traumatic losses of people, property, and security in one's life. Anxiety about life and a loss of security are the core issues. As a result, professional counselors and therapists can determine the necessary treatments for survivors to recover. Establishing long-term partnerships with community organizations can also help build resilience in a church, its leadership, members, and volunteers, who are crisis responders, can minimize a disaster's devastating and stressful impact on survivors.

## Grief and Loss

Losing a loved one, such as a spouse, unborn child, born child, relative, friend, or even a pet, is devastating when it was someone that was near and dear to you. Grief is not something you get over; it's something you work through. Notably, losing a loved one can cause a person to feel numb, lost, hopeless, and in severe cases, suicidal. So, it is crucial for a person who is mourning the loss of a loved one to accept the loss before they can work through adjusting to their life without the person. Because some cultures do not process grief the same way. Based on a person's belief system, some cultures shun away from grieving as a sign of strength when sadly, it is damaging to a person's soul. Because it is unnatural not to release pain through tears and talking to others to get through it. Each individual person has their own way of getting through their grief work. That is why it is crucial if you are experiencing grief and loss, do not allow someone to shame you or be critical towards your grieving process, as long as you are not bringing harm to yourself. Do not allow anyone to tell you that you need to be strong. Grieving is not about being strong; it is about being human and allowing yourself to process pain healthily.

Also, if you are trying to comfort someone who is grieving loss, be sure you are not critical or distant from someone hurting, but instead, show empathy, a listening ear, and being present with a caring attitude, can help someone in the bereavement process one's pain easier. Some people reminiscence of special times they shared with the deceased person or pet. Another way someone tries to cope with the death of a loved one, is by looking over photos they shared of happy memories or a clothing item that makes them feel near during the grief stages stated above. Others hear a song or go to a particular place that reminds them of their loved one, and they become emotional and weep. Don't feel bad. Take time to mourn your loved one. Ecclesiastes 3:4 (KJV) says in the seasons of life, there is "A time to weep, and a time to laugh; a time to mourn, and a time to dance." So, remember, no one can tell you how to grieve, but they can provide healthy support by being present with you in your time of grief, showing empathy, and sharing encouragement for your healing process. That is why healthy support from others is essential during the grieving process. Therefore, withdrawing from others and dealing with grief alone is never good. It is also never okay to use drugs and alcohol to numb your pain. Again, it is very helpful to surround oneself with caring and empathetic support from family and friends, and seeking mental health counseling, which brings comfort and some healing. It is also helpful to want to make your loved one proud by moving on with your life, one step at a time.

## Spiritual Intervention

Spiritual intervention is essential for helping crisis and trauma survivors cope with grief and loss. In the Bible, the book of Lamentations, the prophet Jeremiah is found lamenting (sobbing, moaning, wailing) with intense emotions and deep sorrow, grief, loss, and pain for those against God and the human suffering of His people, and the need for God's help, comfort, and restorations. For example, in Chapter 3 of the book of Lamentations, many of Jeremiah's words are his tears and how he processed his pain crisis through poetry and prayers to God. But in one part of this passage, he worships God and leans on Him for hope, healing, and restoration. Lamentations 3:54-58 (KJV) prophet Jeremiah says,

> Waters flowed over mine head; then I said, I am cut off. I called upon thy name, O Lord, out of the low dungeon. Thou hast heard my voice: hide not thine ear at my breathing, at my cry. Thou drewest near in the day that I called upon thee: thou saidst, Fear not. O Lord, thou hast pleaded the causes of my soul; thou hast redeemed my life.

Here, Jeremiah pours out his heart and expresses his anguish to God for and is comforted through his expressed lamentations through his tears and sincere words to God. This process of lamenting brings healing to Jeremiah's soul.

Moreover, in Matthew 5:4 (KJV), Jesus taught, "Blessed are those that mourn: for they shall be comforted." Those open to Jesus' love and pray to him can experience his comfort and healing in one's spirit and emotions. Another excellent foundation scripture to hold in one's heart and trust God for spiritual intervention for helping someone withstand crisis and trauma is Psalm 34:18 (KJV) says, "The Lord is nigh unto them that are of a broken heart; and saveth such as be of a contrite spirit." Here is a lovely invitation to seek God in prayer when a crisis victim or crisis responder struggles with intruding thoughts of terror, acute stress, grief, hurt, and fear after being exposed to trauma from house fires or any other crisis. Isaiah 40:29 (KJV) also says, "He giveth power to the faint; and to them that have no might, he increaseth strength." This scripture encourages those who are exhausted by life stressors, challenges, and levels of trauma, to understand how God understands the human frame and the psychological and emotional brokenness humanity faces. Still, God gives supernatural strength and comfort to those who pray to Him and ask for His help, relying on and trusting Him to sustain them and endure life's challenges. Also, one of the fruits of the Holy Spirit is longsuffering. This fruit of the Holy Spirit is a supernatural disposition from God to bear and recover from crises and trauma through His power.

## Poverty

Poverty has been labeled into specific categories to the root cause of it. Poverty happens for three reasons. Either *people* cause their poverty from bad choices, *economic changes*, or *natural disasters*, like weather systems that destroy homes, communities, and cities. Being exposed to poverty life of impoverishment has severe consequences on one's livelihood. This issue has divided families and individuals going through this crisis.

A problem in life that can lead to destitution is a person becoming disabled or gravely ill. This crisis can happen to anyone in the workforce, from a personal tragedy such as a car accident or injured on the job. Taking medical leave or losing mobility to perform one's career can affect someone's wages.

The scarcity of employment is another pertinent reason why poverty exists. Some people become poverty-stricken, whether a person lacks schooling to find a suitable job or career to make ends meet or not making enough dollars. Company mergers eliminate jobs also causes this issue.

Another reason is the progression of technology. The digital age has eliminated people's occupations to electronic devices. As a result, technology and robotic machines have become replacements for doing the work.

How a person manages money can determine if one falls into deficit. Poor budgeting of one's finances can result in losing money to pay for the basics in one's life. Another example of exhausting funds can result in overshopping for material things or charging one's credit card for something that the person cannot pay after receiving the credit card statements, affecting one's ability to manage finances properly. Therefore, people getting a handle on how they budget their finances can prevent becoming homeless, a vagabond, or struggling to make ends meet.

*Effects.* The poverty crisis can also lead to a person experiencing strain, worry, and unrest leading to mental health issues. For families, not living in a secure place causes uncertainty and despair. Poverty has caused people to become needy without enough money to care for themselves properly. Consequently, some people desperate to survive hunger or homelessness resort to breaking the law out of desperation to find ways to survive, while others become ill.

People who suffer from living poor also suffer physical illnesses from lack of food provisions and healthy drinks. Due to unclean living habitations, a broken-down house or living displaced with contaminated walls, rodents, and filth that children or adolescents are exposed to causes severe health problems. As a result, children and adolescents resort to unhealthy ways to cope with the pain and agony of living impoverished.

As stated before, food is an escape from the misery of living in a harsh environment. A lack of food can cause low energy, affecting a person's ability to think, which can affect their mental health. Some youth may express a form of gluttony or greed during school lunches or other social events as a reaction to savoring or hoarding food when they have the opportunity to eat healthily but fear losing it. Adults and youth store up food through overeating is a coping way to escape the dread of poverty.

## Intervention to Poverty

A person changing their mindset from feeling helpless to hopeless is a start. In some cases, those who caused their poverty can re-evaluate their choices and make better decisions to escape self-induced poverty. Self-evaluation is recognizing the cause of one's poverty and guiding them to resources are other steps toward a resolution to helping those suffering lack get rid of poverty from their lives. An example of preventing poverty or eliminating it from one's life can start with those who are disadvantaged to being optimistic and writing a vision board to plan positive goals to pursue as steps to escape poverty. Committing to changing one's thought processes and pursuits from negative to positive can influence change in one's economic status. Also, wanting to be independent of others to save one from poverty and taking the initiative to pursue the right goals, places, and decision-making skills is vital to breaking out of a life of deprivation. This includes eliminating negative associations with people who do not have a plan or vision for their lives and choosing to connect with resourceful people who can help guide and mentor one to the support to help them rebuild their lives intentionally and diligently.

*Education.* Dependent upon one's educational background, a person may either need to complete their education or further their education. Because academic credentials help one experience personal growth, become an asset to corporate businesses, and be more marketable for career opportunities to reduce the risk of poverty. Higher education can deliver people with low incomes from ruin. So it is essential for a person to appreciate and value the privilege of getting an education or additional career training to become more self-sufficient, build resilience in one's character toward a valuable career and adjust to the changes in the economy while remaining financially sustained. Therefore, education is vital role in a successful career path for sufficient income and better living.

*Employment.* Finding work or establishing a career is one of the solutions to eliminate or reduce the issues of poverty in our world. As stated before, a person's chances are higher to become employed after receiving a high school or college education and diligently pursuing work to make a living and not live impoverished. Seeking employment takes determination, and planning to find suitable job leads, locations, and community support systems can heighten one's chances of getting hired and becoming productive. As a result, this is personally fulfilling and is sufficient to take care of one's housing in a proper environment and cover one's basic needs.

*Re-employment.* A new chance of reemployment after a layoff, termination, or other economic reasons can pull someone out of poverty. Your commitment to networking with employment organizations with professionalism and a good attitude increases your chances for re-employment. A person's professional connections, people skills, and reputation increase the chances for one to establish reemployment in sufficient work to provide the core needs for one's life. Overall, poverty is a humanity issue from deprivation of basic needs, finances, safe living conditions, and family support. Many causes stem from society's perceptions, economic injustices, policy issues, educational requirements, and fluctuations in employment possibilities. As a result, those suffering from lack are vulnerable to health issues, legal consequences, broken families, and sometimes death. However, personal ambitions and economic growth providing more job security, spiritual intervention, and empathy from political figures, businesses, and community agencies can help the underprivileged and those in poverty to a place of good living.

## Crimes

Some people have experienced being victimized by crimes that have been a crisis or traumatized them. As mentioned before, abuses and assaults are some examples of being a victim or survivor of crimes. Others have experienced being robbed or robbed at gunpoint, burglary, arson, and terrorism.

*Effects.* Being a survivor of crimes can cause some severe psychological issues. Namely, anxiety, fear, anger, distrust, depression, and suicidal thoughts are some of the effects of world crimes. Realize it is essential that citizens can trust law enforcement and the justice system to protect them from criminals. This is critical for people to maintain their mental health. If the police are criminals and are racists, this puts many lives in danger of mental illness and premature deaths. Some people also resort to becoming a hermit from fear of the crisis happening all over again. So, recovering from these criminal violations takes time and is a long time process for many. Community collaboration among residents and neighbors working with community wellness agencies and churches for support is one of the most considerable solutions to crime prevention, and promoting mental health.

Additionally, social withdrawal is alarming because when residents in high-crime neighborhoods do not feel safe to the point they don't trust anyone, law enforcement, or their community allies, it will be difficult for residents to collaborate with others through block watch meetings or community wellness meetings to find solutions for crime prevention. Notably, community collaboration is essential for positive change to take place in communities to reduce and stop crimes such as harassment, murders, assaults, violence, and burglaries in neighborhoods. There is indeed strength in numbers, which means, a team effort between neighborhoods, community agencies, and law enforcement willing to establish monthly meetings promoting solutions for crime prevention and community wellness and incentives for neighbors (adults, children, and teens promoting safety and health can help produce positive change. As a result, many people can experience mental wellness and physical health because their environment is safe and supports mental health and well-being. When people can trust their communities, especially being able to trust law enforcement not to use discrimination and mistreat certain races in their role of crime prevention, but to uphold fairness of the laws toward anyone as necessary, and not to mistreat the mentally ill, nor reject citizens who have chronically called for help from perpetrators trying to harm them, innocent people can feel and live safe.

# CHAPTER 5

# DEALING WITH CHURCH HURT

Don't let anyone tell you *church hurt* is not real. *Church hurt* is very real. Church hurt hurts! Church hurt is another detri mental dilemma many people worldwide experience which can cause many *mental injuries* and *spiritual afflictions*. Some examples are, being misled or mistreated by a church leader or member. It is one of the most harmful things a person's spirit and soul can experience. This is a crisis of faith for those who share this level of hurt. Because the church is supposed to be a safe place, a place of refuge for hurting and broken people to receive emotional and spiritual support, guidance and direction from a pastor, priest, or church leader, to connect with God, to alleviate suffering in their lives.

*Misled.* Being misled is one form of church hurt. This is when a pastor, priest, pope, or church leader teaches a wrong doctrine that opposes the Bible. Instead, the leader promotes immorality. In other cases, some leaders misuse the church's finances for their personal greed to misusing money set aside to help support the wellness of the church and support the community, helping the needy with necessities. Instead, the leaders scams god's people and uses the money to buy things for themselves. This is wrong, confusing, grievous, and upsetting to true Christians and faithful church members who learn of deceit from a church leader. It's wicked and devastating.

***Hypocrisy.*** Others live in hypocrisy. This means they live a double life. They preach moral excellence from the Bible, but outside of church, they live a sinful life. This is treacherous. For example, some church leaders have been exposed for sexually abusing adults and children outside of church services. The victims either exposed the the corrupt leader's sins to a trusted person or publicly, or the leader was caught by someone else in their immoral behavior. This is sickening.

***Rejection.*** Rejection is also a painful thing to encounter in the church by church leadership. This happens when someone reaches out to the church leader by phone or in person genuinely seeking help with basic needs such as food and finances. Another example is church leaders demonizing mental illnesses such as anxiety, PTSD, and grief and loss, which are emotional problems people experience due to crisis and trauma. Instead of showing compassion and empathy and offering emotional and spiritual support, they shame individuals privately and over the church and blame them for their struggles. In other cases, a broken person seeking counsel and spiritual support is ignored and never receives time and attention from the church leader or anyone from the church. This is heartless and hurtful.

***Betrayal.*** Betrayal is another gut-wrenching pain church leaders can inflict on others. An example is someone sharing a personal matter in confidentiality with the church leader. Later, the same church leader gossips about the person's issue, who they were supposed to respect and maintain confidentiality, and the church leader exposes the person's business over the church. In other cases, leaders can lie about someone in the church regarding a financial or personal matter, and the leader does this to protect their reputation. This is evil and heartbreaking.

***Spiritual Abuse.*** Spiritual abuse is also an horrific and wounding experience church people can go through from church leaders. When church leaders preach God's Word with violence to scare people into living for God, it's *spiritual abuse.* Then there are church leaders who blast church members' business over the church or social events. Other church leaders *brainwash* church members and visitors to fear them instead of God. They want to control the congregation with mind control and speak down to them like they are inferior and not as holy as the church leader.

Consequently, church hurt has caused many souls to stray from God, causing them a *crisis of faith* in their walk with God. Naturally, people look up to church leaders as a representation of God. However, people are human and can error if they don't stay close to God. Some church leaders start off pure but become corrupt over time because of their selfish ambitions, which separated them from God. As a result, they become careless and malicious toward how they treat God's people. However, this is dangerous, and God can see what is happening and is their judge.

Anyone who has been afflicted by church hurt must not seek to harm corrupt church leaders. Instead, they should forgive them and respectfully separate themselves from them. A personal meeting at church with other godly church witnesses is one way to discuss one's concerns and to inform the leader that they need to separate from the ministry because of the distrust and pain a person has experienced. These issues must be discussed from the church member to the pastor or church leader with the right tone of voice and with respect. Afterward, the wounded person must leave the church in peace and never seek revenge against the church leader or slander their name and ministry. It is now time for healing and recovery. This begins in consistent prayer with God, while seeking godly counsel for emotional and spiritual support either from another godly leader at a different church that is authentic, or a counseling agency for healing to begin.

## Church Hurt Two-Way Street

On the other hand, church hurt is a two-way street, meaning church leaders can be wounded by church members as well. Church members, colleagues in leadership, and church visitors can also cause godly church leaders who are genuine for God church hurt. For example, some lie on the pastors or other church leaders, falsely accusing them of hitting on them (flirting) because the church leader will not give them the time or day to engage in sexual sin.

Others are possessed by evil spirits. They are influenced to disrupt and try to stop the great work God is using the church leader to do to help win people to live for Jesus. Other people envy or are jealous of the ministry. So they will try to spread gossip or discord among other church members and leaders, to destroy the reputation of the pure apostle, bishop or pastor.

Just like church members or visitors are emotionally damaged by wicked and heartless church leaders; likewise, it can be just as painful and terrifying for a genuine leader of God to see people they have helped minister encouragement to, provided finances to, and spent time with in ministry, stab their leader in the back with betrayal and drama. This is pure wickedness and certainly causes church hurt and causes some leaders to quit and end their ministries.

## HEALING & RECOVERY FROM CHURCH HURT

The good news is God heals the brokenhearted, and you don't have to stay church hurt. Psalm 34:18 (NIV) says, "The Lord is close to the brokenhearted and saves those who are crushed in spirit." Psalm 34:18 (MSG) explains it even deeper, stating, "If your heart is broken, you'll find God right there; if you're kicked in the gut, he'll help you catch your breath. As you can see, God's Word shows you He is concerned about anyone whose heart is aching from any abuse from a person, especially those you loved and held high regard for, that has caused you heartbreak. It reads, teaches, guides, comforts, and heals you.

Adaptability, rehabilitation, and rebuilding your life are vital for survivors of church hurt crisis to get back to living with some normalcy during recovery. God's power through your prayers for help, comfort, and healing can touch your mind, heart, and spirit and heal you from the pain. God will also teach you to trust Him and not people.

God also can redirect you to a new church for safety, healing, and recovery if you seek Him in prayer and pursue Christian counseling from a community agency or a referral from someone. Jeremiah 23:1-4 (AMP) says,

Woe to the shepherds (civil leaders, rulers) who are destroying and scattering the sheep of My pasture! says the Lord. Therefore thus says the Lord, the God of Israel, in regard to the shepherds who care for and feed My people: You have scattered My flock and driven them away, and have not attended to them; hear this, I am about to visit and attend to you for the evil of your deeds, says the Lord. Then I will gather the remnant of My flock out of all the countries to which I have driven them and bring them back to their folds and pastures; and they will be fruitful and multiply. I will set up shepherds over them who will feed them. And they will not be afraid any longer, nor be terrified, nor will any be missing, says the Lord.

In other words, God has only a few genuine, authentic leaders who serve Him and live pure lives unto God in their private lives and in public. In the same way, Jeremiah 3:15 (KJV) goes on further to say, "And I will give you pastors according to mine heart, which shall feed you with knowledge and understanding." These are leaders who lives unto God in their private and public lives.

So, there is hope and a new path for those of you who have struggled with returning back to church because of church folks wounding you. Nobody deserves to be misled, mistreated, rejected, betrayed, abused, and used by anyone in the church or anywhere in life. You are valuable and deserve to be treated with the utmost respect, especially in the house of God.

Also, for church leaders who have quit the ministry due to betrayal and ungratefulness of their previous flock, God is their healer and restorer. If this is your situation, stay prayerful and seek God's comfort and strength for healing. It is also critical to seek counsel from a circle of healthy leadership for recovery.

## Sin

Another cause of crisis and trauma is living a lifestyle of sin. Living spiritually separated from God causes traumatic human suffering because of a person's choice to engage in sin. Choices people make against God and their livelihood can cause some of their human suffering in the area of sin. Any behavior that is immoral and causes you hurt and others pain is a *sin*. The Bible says, "For the wages of sin is death; but the gift of God is eternal life through Jesus Christ our Lord." As you can see, a person's choice to do bad things will later affect their eternal life in the spirit world. If you are unsure of what sin is, Galatians 5th chapter in the Bible explains what moral excellence to God is and what immorality looks like.

Galatians 5:14-18 (KJV) apostle Paul teaches saying,

> For all of the law is fulfilled in one word, even in this; Thou shalt love thy neighbour as thyself. But if ye bite and devour one another, take heed that ye be not consumed one another. This I say then, Walk in the Spirit, and ye shall not fulfil the lust of the flesh. For the flesh lusteth against the Spirit, and the Spirit against the flesh: and these are contrary the one to the other: so that ye cannot do the things that ye would. But if ye be led of the Spirit, ye are not under the law.

Notably, the *flesh* refers to a mentality or behavior that is sinful. Galatians 5:19 (KJV) first identifies sexual sins which says, "Now the works of the flesh are manifest, which are these: Adultery, fornication, uncleanness, lasciviousness."

Here, these are sins people decide to commit with their bodies. For example, adultery is a sexual relationship with someone who is married to someone else. The world calls it an affair, but this is displeasing to God. It can cause unnecessary crises such as diseases and potential violence or murder between the people in the triangular affair out of revenge and hurt. It takes a wise person not to choose these paths. Later in this chapter, you will be encouraged on how to get well spiritually and for your mental health. Galatians 5:20 (KJV) identifies relational problems with others as, "Idolatry, witchcraft, hatred, variance, emulations, wrath, strife, seditions, heresies." Here, this scripture describes people who choose not to get along with others, wishing them harm through obsessions, hate, debates, division, gossip, and evil prayers. As a result, a breakdown of relationships happens, causing toxic relationships with others, which can cause traumatic experiences of drama that can damage families, friendships, and ultimately one's relationship with Almighty God.

Next, in Galatians 5:21 (KJV), apostle Paul also describes behavioral problems that people struggle with by choice, identified as, "Envyings, murders, drunkenness, revellings, and such like: of the which I tell you before, as I have also told you in the past, that they which do such things shall not inherit the kingdom of God." As you can see, negative behaviors of ill will toward others, killing others verbally or physically, addictions, and rivalries result in choices a person makes. As a result, unnecessary tragedies can happen among people with these issues because these behavior problems stem from bad feelings and relationships with others, with no peaceful resolve.

## DEMONIC OPPRESSION

Remember in the Crisis & Trauma chapter, one thing you read about was the soul: your mind, will, and emotions, and how crisis and trauma can make the soul sick? Comparatively, a person's spirit can also become crushed and not well. The Bible identifies it as the *human spirit having infirmities.* To illustrate, Luke 13:10-13 (AMP) says,

Now Jesus was teaching in one of the synagogues on the Sabbath. And there was a woman who for eighteen years had had an illness caused by a spirit (demon). She was bent double, and could not straighten up at all. When Jesus saw her, He called her over and said to her, "Woman, you are released from your illness." Then He laid His hands on her; and immediately she stood erect again and she began glorifying and praising God.

As stated above, the woman with an illness in this story had a demonic illness that weakened her spirit, which also made her vulnerable to physical sickness.

So, know that there are two levels of being mentally ill. Some people can be mentally ill without demonic oppression and depression. This means a person can struggle with anxiety and panic attacks due to a crisis of physical or sexual abuse they experienced. In this case, this person needs mental health care and spiritual counseling for recovery.

On the other hand, a different level of mental illness can come from demonic oppression and demonic possession. Notably, there is a difference between demon oppression and demon possession. To be demonically oppressed is to suffer from severe sadness and depression from personal issues or unresolved crises. Demonic oppression happens to a person from a spiritual infirmity (demonic attack in the human spirit and soul) or depression, untreated from crises and trauma. When a person experiences a crisis such as sexual abuse, physical abuse, grief and loss, and other involuntary situations that cause them fear, distress, anger, despair, and sadness if a person does not receive spiritual care or professional treatment to heal and recover from these crises, they can begin to experience spiritual weakness and become vulnerable to demonic attacks in their mind and spirit, that life is hopeless with a spirit of darkness and revenge, because of the pain they suffered by the hands of someone else's wicked behavior against them.

Without healthy family support, and professional spiritual care, dark spirits are drawn to people who are spiritually weak and suffer from depression. Consequently, those spirits begin to take over a person's mind, distorting their thinking, causing them to behave violently and do wicked things. Because demons will use the person's sadness to overtake them to feelings of hopelessness and openness to more wicked feelings.

On the other hand, when a person is demon-possessed, this is more than mental illness. This person has yielded to the world of darkness or wicked powers with no defense. Not only is the person's spirit carrying infirmities from lack of relationship or connection with God, but a person develops mental illness because the demonic power begins to control them from their unstable emotions causing this person to become mentally impaired, leading to self-harm and violent behaviors. The person can also be dangerous enough to hurt or kill others. Sadly, this can also lead to *suicide ideation.* So they don't need a professional counselor or mental health therapist at this time. They need spiritual care from a godly pastor or minister to free them from demonic possession using God's power. To illustrate, let's look at how Jesus encountered and helped free a mentally ill child who was demonically possessed. Matthew 17:14-18 (KJV) says,

> And when they were come to the multitude, there came to him a certain man, kneeling down to him, and saying, Lord, have mercy on my son: for he is lunatick, and sore vexed: for ofttimes he falleth into the fire, and oft into the water. And I brought him to thy disciples, and they could not cure him. Then Jesus answered and said, O faithless and perverse generation, how long shall I be with you? how long shall I suffer you? bring him hither to me. And Jesus rebuked the devil; and he departed out of him: and the child was cured from that very hour.

In these scripture passages, the word *lunatick* is a medical term for the mentally ill. In scripture, the word lunatick was not used in a derogatory way but to describe the mental illness condition of someone who needed help. For example as mentioned before in scripture, before the demon was cast out of the child's body, the demon caused the child to be violent. Notice how Jesus' authority and power, in his words called the demon out of the child, and the evil spirit left him, and the child became alright.

Demonic oppression also leads to physical sickness. Jesus

healed many who were physically and mentally sick. Matthew 4:23-24 (KJV) says,

And Jesus went about all Galilee, teaching in their synagogues, and preaching the gospel of the kingdom, and healing all manner of sickness and all manner of disease among the people. And his fame went throughout all Syria: and they brought unto him all sick people that were taken with divers diseases and torments, and those which were possessed with devils, and those which were lunatick, and those that had the palsy; and he healed them.

Look at how Jesus healed so many mental and physical illnesses to bring them to wellness. That is God's will for all of humanity.

Here is another illustration from Mark 5:1-5 (AMP), which says,

They came to the other side of the sea, to the region of the Gerasenes. When Jesus got out of the boat, immediately a man from the tombs with an unclean spirit met Him, and the man lived in the tombs, and no one could bind him anymore, not even with chains. For he had often been bound with shackles [for the feet] and with chains, and he tore apart the chains and broke the shackles into pieces, and no one was strong enough to subdue and tame him. Night and day he was constantly screaming and shrieking among the tombs and on the mountains, and cutting himself with [sharp] stones.

Notice how the demonic-possessed man was using stones to cut himself. It is a typical behavior of people who suffer with depression and suicidal thoughts to cut themselves, punish and destroy themselves, because a demon spirit is controlling them to be violent, feel self-hate to lead to death.

Mark 5:6-14 (AMP) continues the story about the possessed demonic man saying,

Seeing Jesus from a distance, he ran up and bowed down before Him [in homage]; and screaming with a loud voice, he said, What business do we have in common with each other, Jesus, Son of the Most High God? I implore you by

God [swear to me], do not torment me! For Jesus had been saying to him, "Come out of the man, you unclean spirit!" He was asking him, "What is your name?" And he replied, "My name is Legion; for we are many." And he began begging Him repeatedly not to send him out of the region. Now there was a large herd of pigs grazing there on the mountain. And the demons begged Him, saying. "Send us to the pigs so that we may go into them!" Jesus gave them permission. And the unclean spirits came out [of the man] and entered the pigs. The herd, numbering about two thousand, rushed down the steep bank into the sea; and they were drowned [one after the other] in the sea. The herdsmen [tending the pigs] ran away and reported in the city and in the country. And the people came to see what had happened. They came to Jesus and saw the man who had been demon-possessed sitting down, clothed and in his right mind, the man who had [previously] had the "legion" [of demons]; and they were frightened.

Notice, as stated above, the man freed from demonic possession, the scripture said he became (clothed and in his right mind). So apparently, before Jesus' exorcism towards the man, the man was not clothed, which is another sign of demonic possession. Other signs are lewdness or being dressed in immoral clothing. Again, this is demonic possession.

So, like Jesus, help free people from demonic oppression and possession, only a godly pastor or counselor who carries the power of God can also cast out demon spirits from people's bodies. After a person is free from demonic possession, the person's mind is clear and sober and able to make sound decisions, like allowing God into one's heart and life for spiritual liberation and continued spiritual care from a godly leader. Getting professional care to work out emotional issues will also be helpful for the person's improved mental health.

Surely, you do not want to choose to live in the way of darkness. So, when you don't engage in sinful behaviors, you prevent certain calamities from happening to you. John 3:16 (KJV) says, "For God so loved the world, that he gave his only begotten Son, that whosoever believeth in him should not perish, but have everlasting life." God's love and grace will help redeem you from wicked powers. John 14:6 (KJV) says, "Jesus saith unto him, I am the way, the truth, and the life: no man cometh unto the Father, but by me." In other words, to living life to the fullest in God's joy and blessings, surrendering your human spirit to God through accepting Jesus Christ into your heart to be your Lord and Savior is the beginning of your life transformation. No other religion or faith outside of Jesus will make you spiritually, psychologically, and physically whole. Because God created every human life, and Jesus was sent to save us from our sins through his purity and obedience to God, Jesus is our way, truth, and life to reconnect and live for our God, as God's original plan was, since He created humanity, which is explained in the book of Genesis in the Bible. So, God has a greater purpose for you. He is the only one through Jesus who can empower you to live a moral life. You can only do this through repentance of sin to God in prayer and accepting Jesus into your heart through believing and confessing he is your Lord and Savior. Remember, Romans 10:9 (KJV) says, "That if thou shalt confess with thy mouth the Lord Jesus, and shalt believe in thine heart that God hath raised him from the dead, thou shalt be saved." Afterward, ask for God's Holy Spirit to live in you to empower you to resist sin. As stated before, choosing to live a pure life in God leads your life to blessings and good living. Jesus is your life. He also empowers your mental health through his Words from the scriptures and His voice spoken directly to you as well through God's Holy Spirit. John 6:63 (KJV) Jesus taught, "It is the spirit that quickeneth; the flesh profiteth nothing: the words that I speak unto you, they are spirit, and they are life." As you can see, God's Words of holiness and purity through scriptures speak life to your spirit, and you read them aloud and live by them.

God also speaks to us directly to our human spirit with His

voice, Jesus, through other people on the earth and His angels from the invisible world. As mentioned in Chapter 3, God also speaks to us in dreams through symbols and images as metaphors of special messages to guide our lives. A later chapter will discuss in greater depth how God speaks to humanity through dreams and visions.

Furthermore, please understand that giving your life to God does not stop you from facing challenges and trials in your life. John 16:33 (KJV) Jesus spoke a crucial message to his disciples and humanity before he ascended to heaven after his resurrection, stating, "These things I have spoken unto you, that in me ye might have peace. In the world ye shall have tribulation: but be of good cheer; I have overcome the world." Notably, the main tribulation Jesus referred to was the spiritual war of good versus evil among humanity and government systems in the world. Not saying you will not experience crises in life, but living for Jesus will reduce troubles and stop them from traumatizing you. Having Jesus Christ allows you to prevent certain crises from happening to you because you choose not to sin, which eliminates judgment and certain ripple effects from sin from happening to you. Living for Jesus also empowers you spiritually and mentally to bear through any challenges with great supernatural strength, resilience, and peace. Living for Jesus also allows you to experience spiritual and material blessings you never would have experienced without him.

# CHAPTER 6

# MOVIE CASE STUDY

## Movie Review

One movie that was powerful in transforming different characters who experienced various tragedies was *"Indivisible."* This heartwarming film was a true story about military families overcoming grief and loss and post-traumatic stress from military men in marriages. One, in particular, had a guy named Darren Turner who was married to a lady named Heather, with children, a Christian family who began to face struggles after Darren Turner was deployed to Baghdad for 15 months to be a military Chaplain for a special operations army base. Prior to his deployment, his family was the typical family that functioned well. They all loved each other dearly. One of their neighbors they recently met with was another couple named Michael Lewis (an army soldier), who was married to a lady named Tonya, and this role was played by the famous actress (Tia Mowry). So this couple struggled with their marriage relationship, due to her spouse's post-traumatic stress issues of anger from his previous deployments in the army. Chaplain Darren is suddenly called to deployed to a military base for ministry. In preparation for Michael Lewis and Chaplain Darren's new deployment assignment together, Michael Lewis noticed Chaplain Darren in the backyard near their homes, and had small talk. Michael Lewis noticed how spiritual and hopeful Chaplain Darren appeared about their deployment assignment and Michael Lewis was annoyed. Michael Lewis warns Chaplain

Darren that the army will change his attitude from hopeful to bitterness toward God, his role as a Chaplain, and life.

Chaplain Darren and Michael Lewis later arrived in Bagdad at their military bases. Chaplain Darren is introduced to the military bases with a hopeful attitude and zeal about God being the source and help for their lives during military battles. One of the guys named, Lance Bradley, was initially cynical at first about Chaplain Darren's faith. Chaplain Darren also meets an African American lady sergeant named Shonda Peterson, who is honorable in serving her country but struggles internally being a single mom, separated from her son, whom she had to leave behind with her mom for deployment and she feels like a bad parent. However, Chaplain Darren gave out Christian coins, small Bibles, and beef jerky food to encourage military personnel, and he would pray with military staff.

In the meantime, back at home, where Chaplain Darren and Michael Lewis's wives were, Heather and Tonya supported one another. Heather had a Family Readiness support group for women who had lost their spouses. A lady named Amanda is younger, (who is married to Lance Bradley) from Chaplain Darren's base. Heather decides to offer help for friendship and emotional support. They also worked together to prepare care food packages to send to military staff.

## Turning Point

One of the scenes that warrants reflection is a turning point in the movie, when Chaplain Darren and his army base all begin to experience unexpected combat of bombs dropping and gunfire all around them, as they all run and fight for their lives. After exposure to casualties, one was Chaplain Darren being handed a dead little girl casualty and seeing wounded or dead people during military combat and exposure to bombings begin to mentally affect Chaplain Darren's mental health. Although Chaplain did self-recorded videos to send to his wife to process his experience in the military, later, his phone calls with his wife he began to speak with frustration and trembling hands, and his phone calls had changed from pleasant check-ins to seeming distracted and detached from his wife, and home life.

Chaplain Darren later conducted memorial talks in the military platoons. He would relate the soldiers sacrificing their lives for their country and others like Jesus sacrificing his life for humanity. Sadly, he lost a close friend, and another was severely injured, which shook Chaplain Darren's faith in God. Consequently, mental and emotional (PTSD) post-traumatic stress disorder was setting in for Chaplain Darren.

## Professional Critique

Since the main character, Chaplain Darren character had changed from being a kind person and a man of faith to stressed and bitter, there are a few professional critiques to focus on that correlate with his thought processes and the condition of mental injury he experienced in the military, that troubled his home life after he returned from the army back to his family.

### THE RETURN HOME

Chaplain Darren was troubled mentally in civilian life after he returned home. Although he was with his wife and kids, he was not his friendly self. Because of the horrific flashbacks of the combat he had experienced and witnessed casualties of war, including the injury of his friend, Michael Lewis, and the death of his friend Lance, Chaplain Darren was jumpy and reactive in his own home. Heather, his wife, noticed how paranoid and distant her husband was toward her and their children. She also saw him separate himself to sleep on a sofa because he was restless and afraid to sleep. He struggled with hallucinating about bombs locking house windows, being out of touch with his family, missed dinners, and bedtimes. There was one time he broke a drinking glass, injured his hand, and he had intense arguments with his wife about his mean attitude and lack of communication with her. After his behavior got out of control to the point he started yelling at their kids in rage, his wife asked him to leave home to get spiritual care and professional help. If you examine Chaplain Darren's troubling behavior at home, he seemed to be dealing with symptoms of PTSD, Post-Traumatic Stress Disorder. Research shows, signs of post-traumatic stress are reactions of fear, anxiety, hypervigilance, mood swings, and depression.

## PROFESSIONAL CARE

The next scene warrants reflection because Chaplain Darren seemed to also be suffering from a mental health issue called *moral injury* from exposure to war. In other words, a person experiencing moral injury has an internal conviction about participating in a particular activity or moving forward with an action. Notably, in this movie, Chaplain Darren was struggling with a crisis of faith in God, which seemed to be a case of *moral injury* he internally struggled with, along with PTSD symptoms because of the mental stress he suffered doing the work of God in the military to encourage others to follow Him. At the same time, while he lost a dear friend, and saw another one injured. Although God was with Chaplain Darren and used him to help other military personnel, Chaplain Darren didn't understand why God allowed his suffering.

So, after Chaplain Darren leaves home, he goes to one of his mentors named Chaplain Rogers for counseling. Then Chaplain Darren went to a landscaping place as a part of his therapy, where he could get peace of mind and recuperation from the trauma he experienced as a Chaplain around the previous military combat. Working with plants and flowers was a therapeutic activity that made Chaplain Darren productive and able to reflect the growth of his plants to the progress of his psychological and spiritual healing. This was the time Chaplain Darren struggled with his faith in God because of the mental stress he struggled with and the tragedies he experienced from being a military Chaplain. Chaplain Darren was angry God didn't protect his friends.

In the meantime, Michael Lewis, one of the dear friends Chaplain Darren bonded with on the military base, had lost his legs but was going through therapy for recovery. Notably, this is one of things Chaplain Darren was troubled about, God not preventing his friend Michael Lewis from losing his legs. However, while Chaplain Darren was struggling with a crisis of faith and PTSD, Michael Lewis was motivated to get closer to God, and he became grateful for his life and was committed to being nice and decided to be a better father to his children and husband to his wife.

Another scene that warrants reflection is when Michael Lewis decides to pay Chaplain Darren a visit to his landscaping site. Michael Lewis addressed Chaplain Darren's crisis of faith, and expressed to him how he inspired him to connect with God through his Chaplain service in their army base. Michael Lewis also revealed to Chaplain Darren some shocking news. The news was that Michael Lewis was with their dear friend (Lance Bradley) during combat as he was dying, and how he shared with Michael Lewis Chaplain Darren was the reason he gave his life to God and that he saw him die in peace. Michael Lewis said Chaplain Darren impacted Lance and him to get right with God. Chaplain Darren had no clue this had happened because there was a separation period between him and Michael Lewis after combat and returning home while Michael Lewis was recovering from his leg injury in the hospital. This was their first time reconnecting and reflecting on their last military encounter before returning home. After Michael Lewis shared the good news of Chaplain Darren's influence that allowed Lance to die in the Lord, Chaplain Darren's faith in God was revived. This was an inner healing moment for Chaplain Darren and his friend Michael Lewis.

ONE YEAR LATER

Within a year, Chaplain Darren and his wife were counseled by Chaplain Rogers to relive the happy times in their marriage. At first, Heather felt hurt about the distance and silence in their marriage. Then, Chaplain Darren began to open up to his wife about his pain of PTSD from his disturbing experiences in the military and how he loved her and their children. He also began to share his journal with her. As a result, Chaplain Darren's marriage finally healed.

Later, Chaplain Rogers offered Chaplain Darren a new Chaplain role in the military. Then his wife encouraged him to take the new job because they were prepared mentally and spiritually to process the challenges of military combat, the stress, and adjusting from it back to civilian life, with God's help. The President of the United States authorized Chaplain Darren to receive a Bronze Star medal at a special ceremony. Michael Lewis started walking again. Chaplain Darren and his wife continued to help military couples make it through the mental challenges and family changes military couples face, and they empowered them to pull through with God's help and mental health support with resilience.

TRUE STORY UPDATE

Notably, because this was a true story, following Chaplain Darren's success story as Chaplain recovered from PTSD,

Darren served as a Chaplain to the Special Forces for three years. He's a battalion Chaplain at Fort. Bragg, North Carolina.This film was dedicated to the Chaplains of the United States Armed Forces and the soldiers that valiantly serve to protect our freedom (Indivisible movie, 2011).

As you can see, God gave Chaplain Darren healing, a new grace, and resilience to help other military families recover from trauma in the military.

# CHAPTER 7

# UNDERSTANDING THE DREAM AND VISION REALM

D o you know where dreams come from? Some of you may wonder, how and why do you dream? There is a psychophysiological explanation and a spiritual purpose regarding dreams. You must understand the meaning of your dreams and their interpretation because they can affect your mind and govern your life, which in turn can affect your mental health and your spiritual wellness.

Let's look at the psychophysiological perspective first. Based on psychophysiological theory, your brain is still active while sleeping and dreaming. Research identifies that when a person knows they are dreaming, it is called *lucid dreaming*. In contrast, in some cases, while one is dreaming, they are more likely unaware of their surroundings outside of the dream.

However, the dreamer's *subconscious* is alert and aware of the people and events in their dreams. Notably, the dreamer's ability to control certain content in their dreams are connected with their state of mind, and also one's spiritual ability and power, which can reveal their inner strengths and can also be a self-reflection of how they would handle events, conflict, stressors, and problem-solving in their waking life.

## THE PINEAL GLAND

Remember, the *pineal gland* was mentioned in Chapter 3, describing how it works in the brain and its correlation to the spiritual world. Moreover, the pineal gland appears to affect how people sleep, which also allows people to dream. Different scientific studies show the pineal gland has a third ventricle, and it controls sleeping cycles. Notably, sleep is how a person's consciousness changes to no awareness of the physical realm but into another realm. As you can see, the pineal gland is said to arise out of a third ventricle of the brain which is described as a structure within the brain. Notably, the third ventricle appears to be in the same area as the pineal gland in the brain. Therefore, the pineal gland works together within the forebrain to regulate sleep cycles as light changes and to connect humanity to the dream world, the spiritual realm.

Now, let's look at the spiritual side of dreams so that you can integrate psychophysiological knowledge with spiritual insight and understand why you dream and how your dreams play a role in your waking life. The most important truth about dreams is, spiritually, the (dream realm) originated from God. They were intended as God's spiritual messages that go into a person's *subconscious*.

First, realize God has given everyone the ability to dream. Next, there are two types of dreamers. Some dream occasionally, and some dream consistently. Those who always dream prophetic dreams and can interpret dreams are in the Office of a 'Dreamer.' Because God calls the distinction of a 'Dreamer,' to receive special messages to guide and preserve people for His kingdom, a 'Dreamer,' receives consistent messages from God of revelation, mysteries, and future happenings about oneself, others, or world events. Sometimes, 'Dreamers' are also *prophets* or *prophetesses*. Their roles will be explained in a later chapter.

So understand there are reasons why you dream. Again, dreams original purpose from God is to guide and help bring solutions to people's lives and to save them from danger to blessings. They are spiritual messages God created as a stream of communication to the human spirit to reveal problems and solutions from the past, present, or future, to bring healing to people from danger to blessings. Because you are a spirit, God communicates to your human spirit through dreams.

To illustrate, let's look at scriptures from the Bible, from Job 33:14-18 (KJV), which says,

> For God speaketh once, yea twice, yet man perceiveth it not.
> In a dream, in a vision of the night, when deep sleep falleth upon men, in slumberings upon the bed; Then he openeth the ears of men, and sealeth their instructions, That he may withdraw man from his purpose, and hide pride from man.
> He keepeth back his soul from the pit, and his life from perishing by the sword.

Notice how these scriptures explain how God speaks to humanity, whether male or female. One of God's most powerful ways of speaking to humankind is in their dream world by imagery. During a person's sleep, God can help the dreamer focus more on His message to them without life's distractions.

Furthermore, in these scriptures, you may have noticed not only dreams were mentioned, but also a *vision*. They are similar visually, but the experience is different. For example, dreams show metaphors and symbols from God requiring interpretation. In comparison, visions can be experienced during sleep or while awake. Visions usually show images, people, and events in actual form. In other words, what you see, is exactly what has happened, will, or may happen, which does not require interpretation.

Notably, visions can be closed or open visions. For example, closed visions happen when your eyes are closed. Whereas, open visions are when you are awake and can be mutually experienced with others in your environment as a message from God. So, whether a person receives a dream or vision from God, they both are powerful messages from God to communicate knowledge, a warning, futuristic events, or guidance to the dreamer.

Here is another illustration, the story of Joseph, the dreamer in the book of Genesis. For those who know the story, this is just a reflection of the story, but for those of you who are not familiar with this story, let's look at what happened and how his dreams from God played a role in the future of Joseph and his family. Genesis 37:3-11 (KJV) says,

> Now Israel loved Joseph more than all his children, because he was the son of his old age: and he made him a coat of many colours. And when his brethren saw that their father loved him more than all his brethren, they hated him, and could not speak peaceably unto him. And Joseph dreamed a dream, and he told it his brethren: and they hated him yet the more. And he said unto them, Hear, I pray you, this dream which I have dreamed: For, behold, we were binding sheaves in the field, and, lo, my sheaf arose, and also stood upright; and, behold, your sheaves stood round about, and made obeisance to my sheaf. And his brethren said to him, Shalt thou indeed reign over us? or shalt thou indeed have dominion over us? And they hated him yet the more for his dreams, and for his words. And he dreamed yet another dream, and told it his brethren, and said, Behold, I have dreamed a dream more; and, behold, the sun and the moon and the eleven stars made obeisance to me. And he told it to his father, and to his brethren: and his father rebuked him, and said unto him, What is this dream that thou hast dreamed? Shall I and thy mother and thy brethren indeed come to bow down ourselves to thee to the earth? And his brethren envied him; but his father observed the saying.

Here, God was speaking to Joseph in dreams about his future leadership and grace to help his family from a specific danger. Sadly, Joseph's elder brothers envied him because his dreams revealed he would be like a boss over them, and his father, Jacob (Israel), favoring him, gave him a coat of colors. However, the dream was prophetic, and his father held the prophecy in his heart because he sensed it was from God and that it was something special Joseph would do to help their family.

Then, later Joseph's brothers' jealousy and hatred caused them to sell their younger brother into slavery. Genesis 37:23-27 (KJV) says,

> And it came to pass, when Joseph was come unto his brethren, that they stript Joseph out of his coat, his coat of many colours that was on him; And they took him, and cast him into a pit: and the pit was empty, there was no water in it. And they sat down to eat bread: and they lifted up their eyes and looked, and, behold, a company of Ishmeelites came from Gilead, with their camels bearing spicery and balm and my myrrh, going to carry it down to Egypt. And Judah said unto his brethren, What profit is it if we slay our brother, and conceal his blood? Come, and let us sell him to the Ishmeelites, and let not our hand be upon him; for he is our brother and our flesh. And his brethren were content. Then there passed by Midianites merchantmen; and they drew and lifted up Joseph out of the pit, and sold Joseph to the Ishmeelites for twenty pieces of silver: and they brought Joseph into Egypt.

So, Joseph is ripped away from his father and the rest of the family to a foreign land with pagan gods, but God helped Joseph prosper, and although he was traumatized by his brothers, God made room for his gift of dreams and interpretation to grow. This happened after Joseph was wrongfully imprisoned because of a woman's lies. The next part of this story will explain how Joseph interpreted Pharaoh's (the king of Egypt) officers' dreams.

## THE BUTLER DREAM

For instance, Genesis 40:2-13 (KJV) explains saying,

> And Pharaoh was wroth against two of his officers, against the chief of the butlers, and against the chief of the butlers, and against the chief of the bakers. And he put them in ward in the house of the captain of the guard, into the prison, the place where Joseph was bound. And the captain of the guard charged Joseph with them, and he served them: and they continued a season in ward. And they dreamed a

dream both of them, each man his dream in one night, each man according to the interpretation of his dream, the butler and the baker of the king of Egypt, which were bound in the prison. And Joseph came in unto them in the morning, and looked upon them, and, behold, they were sad. And he asked Pharaoh's officers that were with him in the ward of his lord's house, saying, Wherefore look ye so sadly to day? And they said unto him, We have dreamed a dream, and there is no interpreter of it. And Joseph said unto them, Do not interpretations belong to God? tell me them, I pray you. And the chief butler told his dream to Joseph, and said to him, in my dream, behold, a vine was before me; And in the vine were three branches: and it was as though it budded, and her blossoms shot forth; and the clusters thereof brought forth ripe grapes: And Pharaoh's cup was in my hand: and I took the grapes, and pressed them into Pharaoh's cup, and I gave the cup into Pharaoh's hand. And Joseph said unto him, This is the interpretation of it: The three branches are three days: Yet within three days shall Pharaoh lift up thine head, and restore thee unto thy place: and thou shalt deliver the Pharaoh's cup into his hand, after the former manner when thou wast his butler.

As you can see, Joseph interpreted another man's dream regarding his freedom out of prison and getting his job back with the Pharaoh within three days.

Genesis 40:14-15 (KJV) Joseph asks for a favor from the butler, saying
> But think on me when it shall be well with thee, and shew kindness, I pray thee, unto me, and make mention of me unto Pharaoh, and bring me out of this house: For indeed I was stolen away out of the land of the Hebrews: and here also have I done nothing that they should put me into the dungeon.

## THE BAKER DREAM

Notably, the baker wanted his dream interpreted by Joseph as well, hoping he would get the same prophecy of getting his job back, like the butler. However, his dream was more disturbing, a metaphorically represented destruction. According to Genesis 40:16-23 (KJV) states,

> When the chief baker saw that the interpretation was good, he said unto Joseph, I also was in my dream, and, behold, I had three white baskets on my head: And in the uppermost basket there was all manner of bakemeats for Pharaoh; and the birds did eat them out of the basket upon my head. And Joseph answered and said, This is the interpretation thereof: The three baskets are three days: Yet within three days shall Pharaoh lift up thy head from off thee, and shall hang thee on a tree; and the birds shall eat thy flesh from off thee. And it came to pass the third day, which was Pharaoh's birthday, that he made a feast unto all his servants: and he lifted up the head of the chief butler and of the chief baker among his servants. And he restored the chief butler unto his butlership again; and he gave the cup into Pharaoh's hand: But he hanged the chief baker: as Joseph had interpreted to them. Yet did not the chief butler remember Joseph, but forgat him.

Notice how the butler and the baker sought Joseph to answer their dreams because they were mentally disturbed. The butler's dream was interpreted by Joseph, sharing the good news with the butler, causing him to feel at ease. Sadly, the baker's end was also prophesied, and his dream happened the way Joseph interpreted it. However, the butler did not mention Joseph for a season to the Pharaoh. A while later, he did because of Pharaoh's troubling dreams. This part of the story is significant because dreams are not only messages from God, it impacts one's mental health and spiritual wellness.

## Pharaoh's Dream

Later, Joseph hears about Pharaoh's dreams about the future famine of Egypt. Notably, Joseph's dream as a young boy of his sheaves bowing to his brother finally begins to unfold.

To illustrate, Genesis 41:8-14 (KJV) says,

> And it came to pass in the morning that his spirit was troubled; and he sent and called for all the magicians of Egypt, and all the wise men thereof: and Pharaoh told them his dream; but there was none that could interpret them unto Pharaoh. Then spake the chief butler unto Pharaoh, saying, I do remember my faults this day: Pharaoh was wroth with his servants, and put me in ward in the captain of the guard's house, both me and the chief baker: And we dreamed a dream in one night, I and he; we dreamed each man according to the interpretation of his dream. And there was with us a young man, an Hebrew, servant to the captain of the guard; and we told him, and he interpreted to us our dreams; to each man according to this dream he did interpret. And it came to pass, as he interpreted to us, so it was; me he restored unto mine office, and him he hanged. Then Pharaoh sent and called Joseph, and they brought him hastily out of the dungeon: and he shaved himself, and changed his raiment, and came in unto Pharaoh.

So, the scriptures further explain Pharaoh's dream was about skinny and fat animals and what seemed to be corn that became scarce in the dream.

> Genesis 41:25-37 (KJV) says, And Joseph said unto Pharaoh, The dream of Pharaoh is one: God hath shewed Pharaoh what he is about to do. The seven good kine are seven years; and the seven good ears are seven years: the dream is one. And the seven thin and ill favoured kine that came up after them are seven years; and the seven empty ears blasted with the east wind shall be seven years of famine. This is the thing which I have spoken unto Pharaoh: What God is about to do he sheweth unto Pharaoh. Behold, there come seven years of great plenty throughout all the land of Egypt: And there shall arise after them seven years of famine; and all the plenty shall be forgotten in the land of Egypt; and the famine shall

consume the land; And the plenty shall not be known in the land by reason of that famine following; for it shall be very grievous. And for that the dream was doubled unto Pharaoh twice; it is because the thing is established by God, and God will shortly bring it to pass. Now therefore let Pharaoh look out a man discreet and wise, and set him over the land of Egypt. Let Pharaoh do this, and let him appoint officers over the land, and take up the fifth part of the land of Egypt in the seven plenteous years. And let them gather all the food of those good years that come, and lay up corn under the hand of Pharaoh, and let them keep food in the cities. And that food shall be for store to the land against the seven years of famine, which shall be in the land of Egypt; that the land perish not through the famine. And the thing was good in the eyes of Pharaoh, and in the eyes of all his servants.

As you can see, God allowed Joseph to decode Pharaoh's dreams about the future of Egypt's economy and the coming famine. Notice God used symbolic images of lean animals and corn blowing in the wind to communicate this message to the ruler of Egypt to preserve his life and the country. Hearing messages from God is all a part of the warnings from life-threatening situations for mental wellness.

Next, Genesis 41:38-44 (KJV) says, And Pharaoh said unto his servants, Can we find such a one as this is, a man in whom the Spirit of God is? And Pharaoh said unto Joseph, Forasmuch as God hath shewed thee all this, there is none so discreet and wise as thou art: Thou shalt be over my house, and according unto thy word shall all my people be ruled: only in the throne will I be greater than thou. And Pharaoh said unto Joseph, See, I have set thee over all the land of Egypt. And Pharaoh took off his ring from his hand, and put it upon Joseph's hand, and arrayed him in vestures of fine linen, and put a gold chain about his neck; And he made him to ride in the second chariot which he had;

> and they cried before him, Bow the knee: and he made him ruler over all the land of Egypt. And Pharaoh said unto Joseph, I am Pharaoh, and without thee shall no man lift up his hand or foot in all the land of Egypt.

Look at how Joseph's dream from childhood continues to unfold of him being put into the position of ruler-ship first before reuniting with his brothers, father, and other family later in this story. Because later in Genesis 42nd Chapter, the Bible describes how the famine from Egypt was also happening in Canaan, where Joseph's family lived. As a result, his brothers were forced to get to Egypt to get food supplies and survive the famine, and guess who they will see helping them; It will be Joseph. So nearing the end of this story which completed Joseph's childhood dream, Genesis 42:6-10 (KJV) says,

> And Joseph was the governor over the land, and he it was that sold to all the people of the land: and Joseph's brethren came, and bowed down themselves before him with their faces to the earth. And Joseph saw his brethren, and he knew them, but made himself strange unto them, and spake roughly unto them; and he said unto them, Whence come ye? And they said, From the land of Canaan to buy food. And Joseph knew his brethren, but they knew not him. And Joseph remembered the dreams which he dreamed of them, and said unto them, Ye are spies; to see the nakedness of the land ye are come. And they said unto him, Nay, my lord, but to buy food are thy servants come.

Do you see how Joseph's dream happens years later, just as God showed him? As you can probably tell, Joseph was either prophetic or a prophet. Remember, some people who receive dreams from God may not be a prophet but prophetic. However, Numbers 12:6 (KJV) says, "And he said, Hear now my words: If there be a prophet among you, I the Lord will make myself known unto him in a vision, and will speak unto him in a dream." In other words, prophets speak God's mind. They are His voice to the world. This is one of the callings and purposes of a prophet, whether male or female. Notably, some theologians believe Joseph was a prophet; others believe he was prophetic.

To continue Joseph's story, reuniting with his family, Genesis chapters 45-47 (KJV) explains how Joseph later reveals himself to his brothers, forgives them, and has them move with their father, Jacob (Israel), whom he reunites with. Then Joseph takes care of his family and his brothers. Wow! God helped preserve this family. Even Joseph and his father's mental anguish from being a part for many years and Jacob believing his son to be dead, Jacob becomes revived once he learns Joseph is alive and can see him again. The work of God's voice in the form of dreams brought healing and recovery to this family.

## The Birth of Wisdom

Another story in the Bible regarding the power of dreams from God and how these encounters established a mental health manual of wisdom was the story of King Solomon, King David's son. But first, let's look at 2 Chronicles 1:7-12 (KJV) states,

> In that night did God appear unto Solomon, and said unto him, Ask what I shall give thee. And Solomon said unto God, Thou hast shewed great mercy unto David my father, and hast made me to reign in his stead. Now, O Lord God, let thy promise unto David my father be established: for thou hast made me king over a people like the dust of the earth in multitude. Give me now wisdom and knowledge, that I may go out and come in before this people: for who can judge this thy people, that is so great? And God said to Solomon, Because this was in thine heart, and thou hast not asked riches, wealth, or honour, nor the life of thine enemies, neither yet hast asked long life; but hast asked wisdom and knowledge for thyself, that thou mayest judge my people, over whom I have made thee king: Wisdom and knowledge is granted unto thee; and I will give thee riches, and wealth, and honour, such as none of the kings have had that have been before thee, neither shall there any after thee have the like.

There are two important points to look at from these passages of scripture. One is God visited Solomon in the form of a dream. God spoke to his human spirit to inquire about his heart's desire.

God cared about Solomon's well-being, so He talked to him in his dream to help bring hope and peace to Solomon's life. As a result, not only was Solomon given material wealth, but he was also given the gift of *wisdom,* to have sound judgment, perception, and ability to make sound decisions and solve problems.

The second point is the wisdom God granted Solomon is a great part of one's mental health and spiritual wellness. Wisdom is God's mind. Wisdom is an excellent guide on how to make the right choices in one's vitality. Later in this book will be more discussion about the benefits of wisdom for your spiritual, mental, and physical wellness. Hence, the book of Proverbs, recorded and written by Solomon in the Bible is timeless and still being used by Christians and others worldwide. So realize the importance of dreams and visions from God for your well-being.

Additionally, the conception of Jesus was another powerful historical event that happened to his mother, Mary, revealed first in a dream. To illustrate,
Matthew 1:18-25 (KJV) says,

> Now the birth of Jesus Christ was on this wise: When as his mother Mary was espoused to Joseph, before they came together, she was found with child of the Holy Ghost. Then Joseph her husband, being a just man, and not willing to make her a publick example, was minded to put her away privily. But while he thought on these things, behold, the angel of the Lord appeared unto him in a dream, saying, Joseph, thou son of David, fear not to take unto thee Mary thy wife: for that which is conceived in her is of the Holy Ghost. And she shall bring forth a son, and thou shalt call his name JESUS: for he shall save his people from their sins. Now all this was done, that it may be fulfilled which was spoken of the Lord by the prophet, saying, Behold, a virgin shall be with child, and shall bring forth a son, and they shall call his name Emmanuel, which being interpreted is, God with us. Then Joseph being raised from sleep did as the angel of the Lord had bidden him, and took unto him

his wife: And knew her not till she had brought forth her firstborn son: and he called his name JESUS.

See how Jesus, our Lord, and Saviour, was brought into the world. God was careful how He communicated to his parents, Mary and Joseph, for the guidance, safety, and well-being and them and their new Son, Jesus. God knew Jesus was a gift to the world and how his birth would change many people's lives, even through this generation today, and many more to follow until the end of time.

God continues to speak to His people in dreams for their protection and well-being. Again, Numbers 12:6 (KJV) says, "And he said, Hear now my words: If there be a prophet among you, I the Lord will make myself known unto him in a vision, and will speak unto him in a dream." This scripture is also true today.

Similarly, Acts 2:17-18 (KJV) says,

And it shall come to pass in the last days, saith God, I will pour out of my Spirit upon all flesh: and your sons and your daughters shall prophesy, and your young men shall see visions, and your old men shall dream dreams: And on my servants and on my handmaidens I will pour out in those days of my Spirit; and they shall prophesy.

## Observer vs. Participant Dreamer

Did you know that a person's thoughts can produce certain dreams? Focus and reflection on specific thoughts before sleep also formulate dreams. Moreover, you do not have to be a prophet for God to visit you in dreams. God speaks to people in dreams whenever He wants.

Notably, you are either an *observer* or a *participant* in dreams. The observer usually dreams about someone God wants to reveal something to the dreamer about. Notably, when a person participates in a dream, it is also considered a dream or vision of the night. The participant is usually told something about themselves from God in a dream.

Distinctively, a prophet will dream more than the average person and see visions. God's voice is open to speak to His people more often than sinners. God will speak to whomever He wants to help people with direction in their lives for their well-being.

## Nightmares

Nightmares or bad dreams can be terrifying and negatively impact one's spirit and mental health. Notably, people experience bad dreams for two reasons. The first reason is that God will show someone a demonic attack planned or in progress through a dream as a warning about what is happening in the spiritual realm. These dreams are messages from God to be aware of what's happening in your life and the evil forces against you. For example, if a person is the *observer* of sexual activity in a dream, it's a warning from God. In these dreams, God will show your intentions, the motives of others in your dreams, or other spiritual beings performing sexual and immoral acts to pollute your spirit and body against God. Being warned by God about this or any harmful activity in the dream allows you to counterattack and cancel the event shown in the dream through prayer and declarations of dismantling evil powers against you or someone in the dream in Jesus' name.

Another reason a person has nightmares is the satanic attacks happening to the dreamer. This is when the condition of the soul of a person is revealed to the dreamer. When people experience these attacks, it can be because they have opened doors to sinful or immoral behaviors. Some examples are a person engaging in witchcraft and a life of sin in their waking life. Other examples are a person's choices of who they are around, and what they watch on television, and listen to, such as demonic movies like horror movies, criminal movies, or pornography. As a result, demons and devils from the dark world can enter your dreams from open spiritual portals or doors a person opens through sin and ignorance to wicked spirits. What you allow your eyes to view on a regularly will tremendously affect your dreams horribly. One of the most common attacks revealed in dreams regarding the devil's hidden plot and attacks against people is sexual attacks. Notably, suppose a person participates in sex acts in a dream as a *participant*. In that case, it's a demonic attack and a warning about the person's lifestyle or the devil's plan to weaken the dreamer to sin in their *waking life.* Satan aims to stop one's spiritual growth, entice the dreamer to engage in unclean behaviors, and influence lust and sin into people's lives by being around immoral people at demonic events to discourage and stop the person's walk with God.

Another reason a person can experience nightmares is God revealing past crises and traumas that were not dealt with spiritually and professionally. Suppressed memories of disturbing images and behaviors can appear in a person's dreams from their present or past. The dream reveals the area in the dreamer's soul needing healing. Consequently, this person will struggle with insomnia and mental illnesses without prayer and counseling.

## Carnal Dreams

Carnal dreams are another kind of dream related to your day-to-day life. As mentioned before, these kinds of dreams usually stem from activities in one's life. For example, a person could have played basketball all day or watched a game show about winning cars for part of the day. As a result, they dream about it. There is no meaning to these dreams. But God allows them because they are from the subconscious of a person's mind.

However, as stated before, you must still be cautious of what you allow yourself to be exposed to visually, the people you surround yourself with, your environment, and your activities. This caution and discipline will help you to control your dream world and open your spirit to understand God speaking to you through dreams to warn you of the plans of the enemy so you can prepare to guard yourself against wickedness and cancel those dreams with your mouth and speaking God's Word while choosing not to sin or engage with people, places and things that allow the devil to have power to control your life. Therefore, for your mental and spiritual health, you must be careful what you allow yourself to be exposed to visually, the people you surround yourself with, your environment, and your activities.

# Special Letter To Reader

Dear Reader,

As the Author of this book you are reading, God has chosen me to interpret spiritual happenings about myself and others through the realm of dreams. For many years, I didn't understand why I would dream about past, present, and future events regarding myself, some people in my life, or strangers. I didn't grasp the meaning of my dreams until I read the Bible about how God dealt with people in dreams as warnings, revealing secrets of blessings, or just receiving guidance from Him. I also learned how dreams could be a multitude of business of what is happening in one's waking life, which can invite heavenly visitations from God or satanic powers into one's dreams.

I also understand that my ministry as a dreaming Prophetess and 'Dreamer,' of receiving consistent messages from God of revelation, mysteries, and future happenings, and the skill to interpret dreams from growing in my relationship with God and after listening to other godly people with the same experiences of dreaming. This gave me tremendous understanding and wisdom on hearing God, interpreting my dreams for my mental health and well-being, and helping others interpret their dreams to resolve problems in their life.

In summary, I received this revelation from God that although God is the Creator of dreams because the devil is the prince of the air, he can enter one's dreams through thoughts, crises, and activities from your waking life. Just like God created humanity with the intention of them living pure, some people can still become corrupt in their lifestyles. Therefore, don't be confused about your dreams. It is God's will for you to understand your dreams. I advise you to always pray to God for the meaning of your dreams. Seeking counsel from other godly people, particularly prophets and prophetesses, can also help. Again, God is revealing something to you as a warning, blessing, or for guidance. So, when demonic powers enter your dreams, it is a sign that an issue in your life needs to be dealt with spiritually, certain behaviors and activities that need to be dismissed from your life, set free from, and healed. Renewing your mind through reading God's Word, resisting evil, and submitting to God along with prayer is an excellent start to freedom from the dark world and tormenting dreams to a life of peace. Then you will become empowered in your relationship with God and understand the value and power of how God speaks to you through dreams and how it will guide, protect, and preserve your life.

# CHAPTER 8

# SOBRIETY

Sobriety is essential to your mental health. Sobriety is alertness, being awake, self-control, and wise judgment. If you are unaware of who you are or what is happening with you, your mental health will decline, be contaminated, and your life can be destroyed.

So what can cause one to lose their sobriety? Substance abuse is one. People usually indulge in these things as a symptom of a bigger problem. Notably, this answers (why) people engage in drug use and alcoholism.

The (how) people get addicted to drugs, and alcohol is a decision from an individual choosing to engage in substance abuse from the influence of a parent, peer, or society. So, sobriety is a choice. Sadly, when people engage in substance abuse, they let go of their self-control, allowing a drug or alcoholism to control them instead of managing their lives. People often become addicted to a chemical or a substance for two reasons. The first reason is leisure, a way to socialize and fit in with the crowd among peers or colleagues.

The other reason is to numb and suppress the pain of a severe problem in one's life. For example, drugs such as cocaine, crack, and heroin distort one's reality and emotions to deal with actual life circumstances. Instead, the person affected by drugs focuses more on the temporary high than their human pain and suffering. There is no awareness of their present life, only the feeling of the drug that comforts them temporarily. You can't think straight if you are filled with these issues and burdened with these internal weights. Sadly, this is a sure way to mental health issues. Consequently, a person addicted to drugs, in some cases, will sacrifice themselves and their relationships with their loved ones by lying, stealing, and hurting others to get high, not thinking about the consequences of how they hurt themselves, their livelihood, and destroying their personal and business relationships with others.

Alcoholism is equally as bad with different consequences. An alcoholic doesn't just drink socially but, in many cases, in private. There is no restraint to their drinking. Many people who struggle with alcoholism will drink multiple bottles of alcohol, glasses of wine, or beer and become drunk. As a result, they become confused, blackout, and forget their behaviors while in this condition. Some have consequently taken the lives of others by drunk driving. Because their judgment is entirely off, they have lost complete mental and physical control over themselves, altering their personality. Furthermore, people in a drunken condition will either act the opposite of their character or reveal secrets about themselves they would not otherwise tell if they were sober.

From a spiritual perspective, substance abuse addictions can be a family pattern that is infectious to families through generations. For example, one's great-grandfather, who has struggled with this behavior, can influence a pathological pattern for their children to follow the same choice of substance abuse. So, to differentiate if addictions are genetic or learned, addictive behaviors can influence generational patterns, and the mental health effects can affect someone's genetics. It is a spiritual problem that children and adolescents grow up seeing in their homes or family gatherings through holidays over the years that teaches the new generation addictions.

Additionally, have you ever noticed a marketing sign or ad at some liquor stores or restaurants that says, (wine and spirits)? What does the word *spirit* mean in this sense? It means demonic influence and control. That is why the Bible says from Ephesians 5:18 (KJV), "And be not drunk with wine, wherein is excess; but be filled with the Spirit." In other words, God does not want your human spirit and body to be filled and drunk with natural wine. God wants you to be filled and drunk in His presence and power through being filled with His Holy Spirit, your human spirit being filled with God, which is the fruits of the Holy Spirit. Galatians 5:22-23 (KJV) explains, saying, "But the fruit of the Spirit is love, joy, peace, longsuffering, gentleness, goodness, faith, meekness, temperance: against such there is no law." To further explain, the Holy Spirit cleanses, purifies, and transforms your human spirit to the nature of God to experience His love, intimacy with Him, purity, joy, peace, and righteousness so that you won't rely on natural wine for happiness or a sense of peace. But instead, being filled and drunk in the Holy Spirit allows you to be saturated in God's love and wonderful presence, enabling you to experience supernatural dimensions of His glory in your human spirit, soul, and body, which empowers you holistically with (joy over happiness), peace, clarity, comfort, and healing in any area of your life.

Notably, many people argue about if wine is a sin. Some people joke about Jesus' first miracle, turning water into wine. Some people believe the water Jesus turned into wine was fermented differently than today's wine. Furthermore, in scripture, God was talking about not being drunk. For some people, this scripture can be interpreted as drinking just a little wine, but not too much, to avoid becoming drunk. Keep in mind today's wine, in some cases, has alcohol in it, which leads to addiction, headaches, and lapse in judgment.

Listen, God is a God of healing. He will never encourage people to indulge in something that will lead them to temptation, affect their judgment or cause diseases in their bodies. In other words, even if the scripture permits people to drink wine, it clearly says not to become drunk because a lapse of judgment leads to bad decisions and sin. Any sound-minded person knows their temperament. So, mature Christians will not want to drink wine or any alcohol, to avoid the temptation of becoming drunk, which leads to temptations of sin. So understand God will not contradict

Himself or tempt humanity to sin. This explanation is your answer for you to maintain your sobriety, mental health, and spiritual wellness. Again, God wants you to be drunk in His Holy Spirit, your human spirit filled with God, His nature of love, purity, joy, peace, righteousness, self-control, wisdom, and enjoying all of His goodness in relationship with Him through Jesus Christ.

So, you must be intentional about your daily sobriety for your mental health. It is vital to understand that to be sober is deciding to be disciplined with one's behavior; in other words, having a made-up mind to resist and abstain from any substance abuse will cause one to be mentally stable and competent to make sound decisions.

For those of you who have recovered from drugs and alcoholism, this is wonderful! It would help if you now change your *self-concept* and *self-image*. *Self Concept* is essential to your sobriety. In other words, how you see yourself is (your truth). So, understand that you are no longer an alcoholic or an addict. So, do not consider yourself a recovering alcoholic or drug user as if you are still an alcoholic or an addict. Although some professional support groups tell you to confess that, it is better to say that you have recovered because it empowers your spirit and reminds you psychologically that your addictions were your past, not your present. In the support group, you have the right to say, "I prefer to say, I have recovered from alcoholism or drug addictions." Think about it. If you have been clean and sober for over ten years, why would you keep saying you are recovering? No, the truth is, you (have) recovered and continue to work hard at staying sober. You have experienced recovery and restoration of your mental health.

It is also critical that you maintain boundaries for yourself to where you go, who you hang around, and what you consume in your body to resist the temptation of substance abuse. This is a decision you must courageously stand firm with. Notice the key to sobriety is choice and a willingness to change for the better.

Therefore, if you struggle with addictions, choosing to regain control over your life daily is necessary to maintain sobriety. So you must stop buying or stealing drugs and alcohol, even during special occasions, but instead make it your goal to be healthy spiritually, mentally, and physically daily. Then seek immediate help. Don't ever be ashamed to get professional support from a community agency or a church during any stage of your recovery.

For maintaining your mental health, always understand when it comes to substance abuse of drugs, alcoholism, or nicotine use, it is not a disease, genetic, or a default that a person falls into by happenstance. Substance abuse always begins with choosing whether or not to engage in substance use. Before it becomes an addiction, you carry the inner power to resist it. Consequently, society has taught humanity to resort to drugs and alcohol as a coping mechanism when life gets tough. However, this choice spirals into more problems in one's life and becomes destructive.

Remember, do not resort to drugs or alcohol when problems arise. Instead, focus on maintaining your sobriety and your *memory* for your mental health. Recognizing what is evil and what is good is an essential part of your sobriety. Keeping your mind free from evil and worry is sobriety. Know what hurts you and what heals you is sobriety. Understanding your strengths and limitations helps protect your sobriety. Spiritually, asking God for help and strength to get through each day is vital to your sobriety.

# CHAPTER 9

# THE POWER OF FASTING

Fasting is an essential way to *detox* from life's challenges. Notably, fasting is a powerful way to *detox* from the impurities of your human spirit, soul, and body. It is helpful to overcome addictions, bad habits, and destructive behaviors.

So, understand there are different kinds of fasting. Notably, people can fast for their bodies, soul, or spirit. For instance, fasting for the *body* can become a discipline for your body to refrain from eating certain foods and drinking certain drinks for a reasonable time to gain self-control over one's appetite and make sound decisions. You don't fast to kill yourself by depriving yourself of food and water when needed. Choosing to fast is after your physical body is healthy enough to abstain from food and water for a specific time, whether it be hours, a day, or a few days, within a reasonable time that doesn't go outside of depriving your body. Putting this discipline into practice as a lifestyle empowers you to resist the temptation of putting things in your body that harms you and giving in to worldly sins.

A *soul* fast is another kind of fast. In fact, this spiritual exercise of fasting humbles your soul before the Lord. This fast is when you choose to avoid people, places, and things that tempt you to consume alcohol, use drugs, or overeat. Training yourself to refrain from immoral television programs, derogatory music, or any demonic entertainment cleanses your soul in fasting. Then adding prayer to God for His help strengthens your soul to resist engaging in immoral behaviors and activities.

Another kind of fast is for your *human spirit*. Similarly, this fast is a choice to *detox* your spirit from harmful influences and wicked powers. The purpose is to cleanse and sanctify your human spirit from destructive habits, worldly lusts, distractions, and issues of this world and focus on your spiritual life and connection with God. Notably, Jesus fasted forty days and forty nights, but the devil still tried to tempt him to eat. Matthew 4:3-4 (KJV) says, "And when the tempter came to him, he said, If thou be the Son of God, command that these stones be made bread. But he answered and said, It is written, Man shall not live by bread alone, but by every word that proceedeth out of the mouth of God." Notice how Jesus used God's Word to resist (the tempter) the devil's suggestions of Jesus breaking his fast, dying by suicide on the mountain, and worshipping the devil to defy God. Likewise, you build up your resistance to the devil by using the knowledge of God's Word against the devil and speaking it during times of temptation. Also, Jesus teaches humanity not to live by food alone but by God's written Word from the Bible. Scriptures are not just words on a page. They are spiritual food that feeds and empowers your human spirit from God to navigate life's challenges.

Remember, abstaining from food is essential to resisting the temptations, ungodly desires, and weaknesses in your soul. So abstaining from food for a specific time frame builds, disciplines, and cleanses your body to control it from destructive behaviors and builds your human spirit and soul with a resistance to the temptations of this world. As a result, you are empowered with temperament and self-control through God's power working in you. So when you fast, it does not mean you will not feel tempted at times. However, fasting builds your human spirit and body to resist temptation. It's a process that will strengthen your spirit through time to avoid putting harmful things in your body or participating in immoral things. God is your help. Lean on Him daily in prayer and reading Bible scriptures is one of the most powerful ways to help discipline you to resist temptation and help you to overcome addictions in life.

Professional counseling and support groups are also beneficial in continuing your path of recovery and resilience. Ecclesiastes 4:9-10 (KJV) states,

Two are better than one; because they have a good reward for their labour. For if they fall, the one will lift up his fellow: but woe to him that is alone when he falleth; for he hath not another to help him up.

As you can see, having healthy support from others is vital to your healing path. Having accountability to someone who cares about you that is well holistically will encourage you to get well and stay well also. Listening to mental health strategies from counselors and others' shared stories will guide and encourage you to press forward on a healthy path on your healing journey. This book will share more about the benefits of counseling support in another chapter.

# CHAPTER 10

# THE SECRET POWER OF FOODS

Did you know that certain foods improve your mental health and spiritual wellness? God made food to alert your brain and thinking patterns to sharpen your spiritual alertness. He also made certain foods to strengthen your human spirit and physical body to function healthily, even through the most challenging times.

Furthermore, in the Bible, a prophet named Elijah, was strengthened by special food after he ran for his life to avoid being killed by the wicked queen, Jezebel, who despised prophets of God and were against her idol worship. She wanted to avenge the evil prophets Elijah had slain. So she sent out a threat against his life. This made Elijah feel like ending his life, similar to feeling suicidal. However, God divinely intervened with food to comfort and strengthen Elijah's spirit, soul, and body to overcome depression. To illustrate, 1 Kings 19:1-8 (KJV) says,

And Ahab told Jezebel all that Elijah had done, and withal how he had slain all the prophets with the sword. Then Jezebel sent a messenger unto Elijah, saying, So let the gods to do to me, and more also, if I make not thy life as the life of one of them by to morrow about this time. And when he saw that, he arose, and went for his life, and came to Beersheba, which belongeth to Judah, and left his servant there. But he himself went a day's journey into the wilderness, and came and sat down under a juniper tree: and he requested for himself that he might die; and said, It is enough; now, O Lord, take away my life; for I am not better than my fathers. And as he lay and slept under a juniper tree, behold, then an angel touched him, and said unto him, Arise and eat. And he looked, and, behold, there was a cake baken on the coals, and a cruse of water at his head. And he did eat and drink, and laid him down again. And the angel of the Lord came again the second time, and he touched him, and said, Arise and eat; because the journey is too great for thee. And he arose, and did eat and drink, and went in the strength of that meat forty days and forty nights unto Horeb the mount of God.

Wow! Do you see how cake (bread) and clean water changed the condition of Elijah's mind and spirit from feeling depressed and suicidal to feeling hopeful and revived? This was a supernatural experience for Elijah, as his body was strengthened to get up and move forward with his life, trusting God for guidance, protection, and joy to continue living. Notably, the angel food from God supernaturally sustained Elijah through a long journey. Wow! Remember, to get out of depression, the first sign of recovery is when a person gains their appetite to eat and drink healthy foods. Likewise, remember how healthy foods mentioned in the Bible empowered people can also strengthen you the same way.

Another powerful example is for those suffering from relationship struggles and loss. King Solomon was given a revelation and secret to receive healing from a broken heart and make himself well again. Song of Solomon 2:5 (KJV) says, "Stay me with flagons, comfort me with apples: for I am sick with love." The (NIV) version says, "Strengthen me with raisins, refresh me with apples, for I am faint with love."

Whoa! Who knew that raisins and apples can help empower one's spirit, soul, and body to get well and overcome heartbreak and grief? This knowledge is a mystery from God. Therefore, consider trying these foods to improve your mental health, spiritual vitality, and strength. If you need to check with your medical doctor regarding preserving your health is also wise to be sure there is no conflict with medication or allergy that some people may have.

However, raisins and apples are healthy foods for anyone to build up their immune system and physical health. Organic is the best kind of food. And if you decide to add raisins and apples to your diet as a spiritual medicine, pray over it and bless your food before you indulge and experience a transformation and healing in your human spirit, soul (mind and emotions), and body.

Clean water refreshes one's body and soul. Comparatively, flowing fresh water is good for one's body and for agriculture for growing healthy foods to maintain the nutrition of humanity and the earth's lands to revive one's spirit unto God. Isaiah 44:3-4 (KJV) says,

> For I will pour water upon him that is thirsty, and floods upon the dry ground: I will pour my spirit upon thy seed, and my blessing upon thine offspring: And they shall spring up as among the grass, as willows by the water courses.

Honey is also another powerful health agent. Its texture, natural sweetness, and nutrients can soothe and heal one's body and soul. Some studies show that honey helps heal respiratory issues and blood circulation. What is more, in the earlier days of the Bible, honey was discovered by a servant of God, Jonathan, the son of King Saul, to bring alertness to his mind and consciousness and strengthen his body. To illustrate, 1 Samuel 14:24-29 (KJV) says,

> And the men of Israel were distressed that day: for Saul had adjured the people, saying, Cursed be the man that eateth any food until evening, that I may be avenged on mine enemies. So none of the people tasted any food. And all they of the land came to a wood; and there was honey upon the ground. And when the people were come into the wood, behold, the honey dropped; but no man put his hand to his mouth: for the people feared the oath. But Jonathan heard not when his father charged the people with the oath: wherefore he put forth the end of the rod that was in his hand, and dipped it in an honeycomb, and put his hand to this mouth; and his

eyes were enlightened. Then answered one of the people, and said, Thy father straitly charged the people with an oath, saying, Cursed be the man that eateth any food this day. And the people were faint. Then said Jonathan, My father hath troubled the land: see, I pray you, how mine eyes have been enlightened, because I tasted a little of this honey.

Whoa! Here is a secret revealed about honey. It gives you mental alertness or sharpness and spiritual awareness.

Similarly, Matthew 3:4 (KJV) shares how John the Baptist enjoyed honey with locusts. It reads, "And the same John had his raiment of camel's hair, and a leathern girdle about his loins; and his meat was locusts and wild honey." Notably, honey gives nutrients to the body and can help cleanse the blood and regulate it, restores energy, and relaxes it, which benefits a person's soul and spirit to feel energized and strengthened. It is an ancient remedy to aid in one's mental health and spiritual wellness.

Moreover, honey is also compared to the Word of God. Psalm 119:103 (KJV) says, "How sweet are thy words unto my taste! yea, sweeter than honey to my mouth!" The psalmist was comparing God's Word and His messages like the nourishment and flavor of honey. It vitalizes a person's spirit, soul, and body. Similarly, Proverbs 16:23-24 (KJV) says, "The heart of the wise teacheth his mouth, and addeth learning to his lips. Pleasant words are as an honeycomb, sweet to the soul, and health to the bones." Wow! Amen to that! Remember always to double-check with your medical doctor for foods and drinks best suitable for you based on your current health condition and needs, and ultimately, let God be your guide.

# CHAPTER 11

# THE POWER OF IMAGINATION

The ability to see things and create images in the mind beyond the human senses is a powerful ability for a human being to use. Notice the word *image* is within the word *imagine* in the word. Imagination plays an integral part in your mental health. Imagination is a power that God gave humanity to have, to see beyond the natural realm into the spiritual realm for hope, guidance, and drive in one's life. Your imagination works simultaneously with your thought life. It is crucial to discipline your mind to have the proper knowledge, truths, and information about different matters in life while protecting it from wrong beliefs and negative words and experiences. Obtaining the right information is critical to use your imagination and guarding it from psychological and spiritual issues. How you use your imagination will determine your state of mind and mental health.

An area of imagination that humanity may struggle with is the innate emotion of fear. Notably, there are two types of *fear*. The *healthy emotion* of fear is a reverence or an honor for God or someone a person has high regard for in their personal life or a prestigious position in society.

Differently, *fear* can also be a *negative emotion* when a person begins to experience consistent feelings of intense anxiety about the unknown, feelings of dread about danger, to feel frightened about a person, place, or thing. Many people consider fear (False evidence appearing real). Fear is real or imagined thoughts. For instance, a person does not have to experience something like picking up a snake to fear it. A person also can experience something like picking up a snake and fear it.

## FEAR EFFECTING IMAGINATION

In addition, people who have been through crises of abuse, natural disasters, and grief and loss may also fear it happening to them again. As an earlier chapter discussed, the anxiety is true in some cases, especially for those who have suffered crisis and trauma. Fear is one area in the mind that many people struggle with in their imagination, in many cases because of past crises and trauma a person has experienced or witnessed. For example, a person who fears flying in airplanes believes they will die on the plane because they fear airplanes. In some cases, the fear stems from the *secondary trauma* of hearing about or witnessing someone else dying on the airplane. So this person has psychologically developed a fear of flying in planes. Notably, this person has already imagined over and over in one's mind how they will die if they fly in an aircraft. Not only does this person struggle with anxiety and fear, but also lacks faith in their future. This is how one's imagination can affect their mental health.

Additionally, it is more complicated for people who have suffered from crisis and trauma not to struggle with *fear*. This is understandable. Because the trauma a person experiences is a reality, but the trauma doesn't have to keep repeating itself.

## ALL FEAR IS NOT A DEMON

Did you know there are different types of fear? There is the fear (of honoring God). Then there is the emotion of fear. Fear is an *emotion, reaction,* and state of *mind* which can affect someone's mental health if they are overwhelmed with intense fear about their safety. Realize that fear can affect your human spirit but does not always originate from the demonic. For instance, many faith-based churches teach that fear is from the devil because the scripture 2 Timothy 1:7 (KJV) says, "For God hath not given us the spirit of fear; but of power, and of love, and of a sound mind." This scripture has been misinterpreted incorrectly because some Christians and others believe God was talking about just demonic fear. Notably, this scripture needs to be rightly divided. To further explain, this scripture was also God emphasizing that our human spirit should not be fearful of life's problems, and that the human spirit should not be controlled by distorted emotions or the influence of demonic powers. Therefore, God was talking about He didn't create us to live in a state of fear in our human spirit, emotionally or spiritually.

Although known dangers, such as fire, can burn someone or bad experiences over time causes fear to develop in a person's mind, it is not God's will for humanity to struggle with tormenting fear. In other words, God doesn't want people's human spirits to live in constant fear, anxiety, and fright, due to life circumstances and crises and trauma. Therefore, devils and demons are not the *roots* of fear in someone's life. Again, unhealthy fear is an emotion from traumatic life experiences that makes an uncomfortable impression on a person's human spirit, causing one's soul to struggle with anxiety, terror, and intrusive thoughts threatening their safety.

However, the devil can use a person's fears against them by bringing thoughts of dread and terror, so that they can worry about danger and harm based on past crises, experiences, or world crimes and disasters. Demonic spirits can observe how a person reacts to obstacles after they put thoughts of fright in their mind. Knowledge of this is a powerful revelation you may need time to process but it will help you know when your soul is dealing with fear as a mental health issue versus a spiritual issue and how to address each side of it correctly for peace.

## THE CURE FOR UNHEALTHY FEAR

So it is up to you not to focus on the fear but choose faith and trust in God's love and protection. 1 John 4:18-19 (KJV) says,

"There is no fear in love; but perfect love casteth out fear: because fear hath torment. He that feareth is not made perfect in love. We love him, because he first loved us." So trusting God's love for you to care for you in life cures fear of destruction and death. Remember, God Who made you is the same God Who can keep you from destruction. It is easier to understand when you are a person of faith and have already begun a relationship with God. Always know that God's love preserves you beyond your unbelief or faith. Understanding the depth of God's love for you is the power that secures your life.

## PESSIMIST OR OPTIMIST

Therefore, to utilize your imagination in a healthy manner, your beliefs and morals must be pure. Your belief system regarding God, faith, morality, and self-concept will determine how you imagine your future to be in this journey called *life*. For example, there is a difference between a *pessimist* and an *optimist*. A *pessimist* has a negative attitude and outlook on themselves and life. They believe the worst about everything and lack faith in expecting progress and success. However, an *optimist* has a positive attitude and view of oneself, is hopeful, believes the best about one's life, and has the resilience to bear through any challenges and make the best of life with happiness and joy.
A person's attitude is how their imagination will be impacted, based on their attitude about themselves and life, a pessimist or optimist. Also, what you allow yourself to see on television, movies, and hear on the radio, and the people and places that you spend your time with and listen to will shape your imagination about who you can be and what you can have in life.

So you always want to believe the best about yourself and your future. It starts with believing and imagining better than what you see. Imagination is like *make-believe*. Many adults, through generations, have taught their children to imagine themselves being someone great. For example, girls are encouraged to imagine being a princess, young boys a prince on a white horse, or doctor or lawyer later in life. Likewise, adolescents and adults must train and discipline their minds to imagine the best for themselves in pursuing that: a relationship with God, a nice career, material wealth, and lasting relationships. That is why it is critical that you protect your mind from negative images, words, and environments, to avoid contaminating your imagination and pursuits in your life.

There are also other ways to help you mentally train your thoughts and imagination to be healthy. Imagining a peaceful oasis, a restorative place of relaxation, can do wonders for your mental health. For instance, when you need to decompress, it is helpful to close your eyes in a relaxing room or place away from everyone, light some candles, put on some soft nature music, and imagine being in one of your favorite getaways, like at an ocean. Not only can you imagine this, but you can plan for it as a vacation place to enjoy alone or with a loved one, who is suitable for the trip.

Overall, for more severe cases of those who struggle with the emotion of fear psychologically, there is therapy and mental health counseling, and support groups available to connect with for help. Spiritually, a person needs spiritual counseling to reset and renew their mind about risks in life and how to overcome fear. There will be more discussion about professional counseling and spiritual care later in this book. The next chapter will discuss how imagination and meditation work together to empower your spiritual wellness, mental and physical health holistically.

# CHAPTER 12

# THE POWER OF MEDITATION

Meditation is another vital part of developing and empowering your human spirit and mental health. Meditation is the art of breathing and thinking. To further explain, meditation is a spiritual exercise to make an effort to clear one's mind of stress and negative things and to focus solely on a particular thought, belief, or event, using one's imagination to transform one's life for the better. In fact, *imagination* works together with meditation. Therefore, meditation is seeing oneself possessing or experiencing what their mind is thinking about intensely.

Meditation begins with a person having a creative *vision* about a belief, place, or thing before they can get to the level of meditation. Comparative to the imagination, meditation is not just concentrating on a new concept, belief, or way of doing things. Meditation also includes using your voice to speak to yourself and tell yourself *repeatedly* a particular area of your life you want to see change will happen and is happening. So, for this process to become adequate for one's mental health, the individual must get into a quiet place to focus, avoid distractions and get calm in one's spirit in preparation for effective meditation in one's mind. The right kind of meditation empowers a person's human spirit to experience peace of mind and clarity of one's mind (part of the soul), to gain peace and make sound decisions. Also, what you concentrate on through consistent meditation, will draw that energy to you, whether wickedness from the dark world or good things from God in heaven, which influences one's actions to successful paths in life. For example, a person's beliefs and knowledge they choose to meditate on as a daily practice about living, one's desires, and ambitions will impact how they live and their future. Notably, some people are so developed in their imagination regarding their beliefs and goals they want to accomplish that their imagination automatically persuades them about the power they have to pursue their desires or prevent unwanted events that can impact the course of their life.

## MEDITATION IS PRAYER

Biblically, God teaches humanity how to *meditate* His Word, which reveals His purpose and goals for humanity, to be well in life and overcome obstacles. Meditating God's Word causes light to enter your human spirit and soul. *Meditation* is medicine to the mind and the human spirit. Psalm 19:14 (KJV) says, "Let the words of my mouth, and the meditation of my heart, be acceptable in thy sight, O Lord, my strength, and my redeemer." Notice here meditation is identified as words spoken and not spoken. Interestingly, doesn't this kind of meditation also remind you of prayer? Woah! That is precisely what meditation is, a form of prayer, whether spoken with your mouth or silently within your heart (a reflection of your soul). Psalm 19:14 (MSG) translation says, "These are the words in my mouth; these are what I chew on and pray. Accept them when I place them on the morning altar, O God, my Altar-Rock, God, Priest-of-My Altar." The word (chew) is mentioned to inhale and eat God's Word. Notably, chewing food, like a piece of bread, is how someone eats, savors the flavor, and receives nutrients from food. It is the same way with receiving God's Word into one's human spirit, soul, and mouth for daily healthy living.

Moreover, Psalm 119:130 (CSB) says, "The revelation of your words brings light and gives understanding to the inexperienced." So God's Word carries power, giving you His grace to guide your life and empower you to overcome. God's Word is not to be looked at as just pages of instructions but as His voice of power to change your life. Here are some examples of powerful words from God that are principles of healthy living that will transform your life forever.

Psalm 1:1-3 (KJV) states,

> Blessed is the man that walketh not in the counsel of the ungodly, nor standeth in the way of sinners, nor sitteth in the seat of the scornful. But his delight is in the law of the Lord; and in his law doth he meditate day and night. And he shall be like a tree planted by the rivers of water, that bringeth forth his fruit in his season; his leaf also shall not wither; and whatsoever he doeth shall prosper.

These biblical truths can transform your life (when you believe), and use them daily. Philippians 4:8 (KJV) apostle Paul says,

> Finally, brethren, whatsoever things are true, whatsoever things are honest, whatsoever things are just, whatsoever things are pure, whatsoever things are lovely, whatsoever things are of good report; if there be any virtue, and if there be any praise, think on these things.

The Message Bible of Philippians 4:8-9 explains it better by saying,

> Summing it all up, friends, I'd say you'll do best by filling your minds and meditating on things true, noble, reputable, authentic, compelling, gracious, the best, not the worst; the beautiful, not the ugly; things to praise, not things to curse. Put into practice what you learned from me, what you heard and saw and realized. Do that, and God, who makes everything work together, will work you into his most excellent harmonies.

Notably, meditation can also include admiration of God's creation of nature, such as admiring the beauty of waterfalls, trees, eagles, butterflies, and how plants flourish. Because God also speaks to us through nature outdoors. Learning to enjoy their splendor and purpose is worshipping God for the beauty of His creation and how it connects you to God, restores your soul, and brings peace of mind. Furthermore, some plants, such as fruits and vegetables, can be discovered to help bring healing to your mind and body. For example, gardening is therapeutic for your human spirit and soul to release stress and connect with God's nature and experience His glory and peace, just like Chapter 6 mentioned for the Chaplain recovering from PTSD, post-traumatic stress disorder. Also, apple or berry picking is healthy for your human spirit to enjoy nature, and eating these fruits improves your body. As mentioned in Chapter 10 about the power of certain foods, God created certain foods from the ground on the earth to help sustain us spiritually, mentally, and physically for complete wellness.

So, meditating on the knowledge of God and His purpose for nature empowers your mind, (soul), human spirit, and body about newness in your life and can persuade you that you are not your past mistakes. As a result, these supernatural discoveries help to transform your thought processes, energize you, and enhance your life. Your self-image is empowered and ignites your faith to believe you are a person of worth, respect, purity, and integrity. So you can overcome any challenges in life through new positive experiences. A powerful scripture to think on repetitiously, to murmur to oneself, and to imagine the transformation is

2 Corinthians 5:17 (AMP) says,

Therefore, if anyone is in Christ [that is, grafted in, joined to Him by faith in Him as Savior], he is a new creature [reborn and renewed by the Holy Spirit]; the old things [the previous moral and spiritual condition] have passed away. Behold, new things have come [because spiritual awakening brings a new life].

As stated above, a *spiritual awakening* happens to the person who opens one's heart to Jesus Christ for a spiritual transformation of oneself, becoming connected to God through Jesus, to live a life of purity, free from being enslaved by wicked behaviors, mental depression, and fearful life. Instead, they are empowered through God's Word to see life differently and better, receive power from God, and experience a new life of power in Jesus. Does this mean you would be exempt from troubles and obstacles in your life? No.

It means you will have supernatural power from God to help you bear through those obstacles but with hope and strength from God. Meditating on God's truths repeatedly by telling yourself, what the scripture says about a matter in your life, will persuade you to align your life to His Word and let it govern your life. Instead of you trying to control everything, God will take over for you and guide you into truth and peace through every circumstance in life.

Therefore, as you continue to read, study, and imagine yourself different and changed for the better, until your behavior and responses are willing to change and begin to change for the better, without a struggle. When you believe it and receive it, mediation at work will impact your mental health and reward your life tremendously as you will witness positive changes in your life.

## Forgiveness

*Self Forgiveness.* If you have sinned against yourself, making bad choices that caused you physical or mental harm, that were also choices against God, learn to repent to God. Repentance is (changing your mindset) about wrongful behavior and abstaining from it. Afterward, learn to forgive yourself. People often know they have made a bad mistake by hurting themselves, but they allow guilt and condemnation to overtake their minds. Some former criminals may struggle with this. However, when you choose to change your ways and stop hurting others, and ask for God's help, you have no reason to continue to carry guilt. Instead, say to yourself, that you are changed, forgive yourself, and choose to make better choices to help yourself and others prevent destruction. As a result, you will experience inner healing, and your mind will heal and be free with happiness and joy.

*Forgiveness from others.* Furthermore, you must also learn to ask for forgiveness if you have wronged someone. Many people are sick in their bodies because they have done others wrong. Whether it was lying on them or stealing from them, betraying their friendship, or abandoning them, once you have realized this and you want to change your ways to become a better person for your mental health

and well-being, it is your responsibility to find the person you have
wronged and apologize and ask for forgiveness. If you need a third
party with you as a witness and for safety reasons, it is wise to ask
another person who is sound, godly, or a professional counselor to
help you make peace with the person you wronged. If the person
has passed away, and you never got things right, this may be difficult
for you to face. However, write a letter for the deceased and read it to
yourself as if they were alive to bring closure and healing to yourself.
This process will help you to gain peace and move on with your life.

***Forgiving Others.*** It is also essential to understand that it can
be tough to forget and forgive the offender when someone has
wronged you deeply, mistreated you, or abused you or someone
you love. Not only is their mistrust but a deep hurt people tend to
feel against the offender. Yet, God teaches us to love our enemies
and forgive. Here's a truth from the Bible that empowers you to
love your enemies through Jesus' power you believe and accept,
from Matthew 5:43-48 (AMP), Jesus taught a higher level of love
and kindness for humanity to live by saying,

> You have heard that it was said, 'YOU SHALL LOVE YOUR
> NEIGHBOR (fellow man) and hate your enemy.' But I say
> to you, love [that is, unselfishly seek the best or higher good
> for] your enemies and pray for those who persecute you, so
> that you may [show yourselves to] be the children of your
> Father who is in heaven; for He makes His sun rise on those
> who are evil and on those who are good, and makes the rain
> fall on the righteous [those who are morally upright] and
> the unrighteous [the unrepentant, those who oppose Him].
> For if you love [only] those who love, you, what reward do
> you have? Do not even the tax collectors do that? And if
> you greet only your brothers [wishing them God's blessing
> and peace], what more [than others] are you doing? Do not
> even the Gentiles [who do not know the Lord] do that? You,
> therefore, will be perfect [growing into spiritual maturity
> both in mind and character, actively integrating godly val-
> ues into your daily life], as your heavenly Father is perfect.

To explain, Jesus was teaching the Jews how to show uncondi-
tional love and kindness to their friends and strangers and those
who wronged them. At the time, salvation was not available to
the Gentiles (Non-Jew) because Jesus had not been crucified
on the cross and resurrected from the grave yet. But, Jesus was
teaching his disciples and humanity his nature of purity unto
God. Of course, salvation is available to anyone who accepts
Jesus as Lord and Savior. According to God, Galatians 3:13-15
(KJV) says,

> Christ hath redeemed us from the curse of the law, being
> made a curse for us: for it is written, Cursed is every one
> that hangeth on a tree: That the blessing of Abraham might
> come on the Gentiles through Jesus Christ; that we might
> receive the promise of the Spirit through faith. Brethren, I
> speak after the manner of men; Though it be but a man's
> covenant, yet if it be confirmed, no man disannulleth, or
> addeth thereto.

Also, Acts 2:17-18 (KJV) after Jesus crucifixion and resurrection
says,

> And it shall come to pass in the last days, saith God, I will
> pour out of my Spirit upon all flesh: and your sons and your
> daughters shall prophesy, and your young men shall see
> visions, and your old men shall dream dreams: And on my
> servants and on my handmaidens I will pour out in those
> days of my Spirit; and they shall prophesy.

To further explain, Acts 2:17-18 (MSG) Bible says,

> In the Last Days, God says, I will pour out my Spirit on every
> kind of people: Your sons will prophesy, also your daugh-
> ters; Your young men will see visions, your old men dream
> dreams. When the time comes, I'll pour out my Spirit On
> those who serve me, men and women both, and they'll
> prophesy.

So, the part about loving our enemies is the same truth Jesus
wanted humanity to live by in the earlier days. He also wants people to live by today. His nature has not changed. God's love is not

like the world, to mistreat people and get revenge against someone who wronged you.

On the contrary, God's love is the greater force against evil. So when a person is treated kindly by someone they mistreated, the guilt will make them feel shame and remorse for their sin. The godly love you show towards a person who has wronged you will allow God's light to shine from within you to that person, influencing them to want to change their evil ways. God's love is a *spiritual principle* and a *discipline* that works to touch the hearts of wicked people, and by His love, transform their hearts to purity and forgiveness.

Allowing God to take over your will and you deciding to apply this scripture to be nice to your enemies may initially seem abnormal and challenging. Your emotions may feel angry and waver at first, but once you have made decided to forgive, in your quiet time, continue to meditate on God's Word as a daily practice over and over until you believe and accept God's Word in your heart. As a result, over time, your feelings will change about the person who wronged you, and in some cases, you may feel pity for them or be prompted to do something nice for your enemy. Biblically and spiritually, this is a supernatural transformation God's Word has done in your mind and your emotions freeing you from bitterness and unforgiveness.

Additionally, forgiveness helps prevent illnesses such as headaches from worry, heart attacks from bitterness, stomach ulcers, or high blood pressure from stress. Forgiveness is not only a decision you make, but it is helpful to meditate on these scriptures daily until you no longer struggle with being kind to your enemies.

## HEALING

Mental illness and physical sickness is a worldwide pandemic that many struggle with and need healing, whether in their minds or bodies. But learning the secret of meditation is a big part of your *cure*.

Proverbs 4:21-23 (KJV) says,

> Let them not depart from thine eyes; keep them in the
> midst of thine heart. For they are life unto those that find
> them, and health to all their flesh. Keep thy heart with all
> diligence; for out of it are the issues of life.

Biblically and spiritually, God's Words are life to your spirit and
mind because He used words to create humanity. Namely, mental illness, addictions, depression, and bipolar conditions, God's
Word can help free you. When you read words of hope and healing from scripture and meditate it constantly every day with your
eyes and speak it with your mouth, your spirit will get empowered
to receive your healing from common colds, diseases, and sometimes, deadly diseases. Also, remember, what you meditate on will
draw that spiritual energy and power to you that will cause certain happenings in your life, from the spiritual realm to the earth
realm. Psalm 73:26 (KJV) says, "My flesh and my heart faileth:
but God is the strength of my heart, and my portion for ever."
Additionally, Psalm 119:28 (KJV) says, "My soul melteth for heaviness: strengthen thou me according to thy word." To clarify, Psalm
119:28 (AMP) says, "My soul dissolves because of grief; Renew and
strengthen me according to [the promises of] Your word." Here,
your soul refers to (your mind, will, and emotions), that God wants
to heal. Notably, you can meditate and pray the scriptures about
healing your soul, which is renewing and strengthening your soul
or anyone you know to recover from mental illness, and also a reference to Psalm 23 chapter, about the Lord being your Shepherd.
Let's look at Psalm 23 (KJV), which says,

> The Lord is my shepherd; I shall not want. He maketh me
> to lie down in green pastures: he leadeth me beside the
> still waters. He restoreth my soul: he leadeth me in the
> paths of righteousness for his name's sake. Yea, though I
> walk through the valley of the shadow of death, I will fear
> no evil: for thou art with me; thy rod and thy staff they
> comfort me. Thou preparest a table before me in the presence of mine enemies: thou anointest my head with oil;

my cup runneth over. Surely goodness and mercy shall follow me all the days of my life: and I will dwell in the house of the Lord for ever.

Psalm 23 is a *timeless prayer* that has helped many people get through calamities, crises, trauma, and hardships for generations and centuries, even in the face of death. These words have helped many people in life bear through many difficulties, as God empowered them with the strength to get through and make it in life despite their challenges. What a powerful chapter to read, study, meditate on, trust, and depend on God to fulfill in your life for your well-being holistically! So connecting with God in prayer spiritually is the most powerful way to heal your mind from mental illness and restore it to mental health.

For physical healing, if the mind isn't well, in many cases, a person's physical health will suffer. In other words, if a person is not physically well, it will affect their energy and mental health. When a person is not treated for mental illness, their physical health becomes affected, which can cause premature death.

Also, when a person struggles with high levels of stress and fear, they can become vulnerable to substance abuse, weakening their immune system and cause physical health issues. Furthermore, some people who don't use drugs or alcohol can still struggle with poor physical functioning, such as low or no energy. In some cases, high blood pressure becomes a problem. In other cases, heart issues, ulcers, and other severe health issues. Notably, from a biblical perspective, a person with health issues is not considered physically sick (because only a soul can be sick before healing). Instead, when a physical body isn't well, it is assumed diseased with a (dis-ease).

There are also cases where people prayed for someone to recover from sickness, but they still died. You may also be asking, what about people who you prayed for or other people prayed for, but they still died? This is a personal and sensitive matter for many people. There could be several reasons why the person still passed away, but there was no failure in God, and God only answers prayers that are His will for each person. Consequently, a person who didn't take care of themselves, which led to their poor health, and maybe the sick individual or the one praying for them may not have prayed in faith, in ungodly environments where people are speaking words of death more than life, after prayer.

In a different way, the deceased wanted to go, although their loved ones didn't want to see them go. In other cases, it was the person's time to go according to God's will. Sometimes, people can go to church to receive healing or a miracle of healing from a man or woman of God through prayer. However, this doesn't happen for everyone because some people do not go to church but still need healing in their bodies.

So, there are many reasons why some people still pass away after a prayer for healing. There are some questions humanity will not always have answers for. Don't stress yourself trying to figure it out for your mental health and spiritual wellness. However, for God's people and those who truly trust Him and don't work against their health, He grants healing when you believe and consistently meditates and speak His word over your life after your prayer for healing. There are many examples on social media and testimonies in research of how God healed people because of their faith. 1 Peter 2:24 (KJV) describes Jesus' healing power to humanity, saying, "Who his own self bare our sins in his own body on the tree, that we, being dead to sins, should live unto righteousness: by whose stripes ye were healed." As you can see, Christians are already healed. They must fight for it against the power of darkness to maintain it.

Therefore, remember, your healing is personal. Don't compare yourself to what happens to others. Trust God for your own healing and remember all the times He has healed you from sicknesses throughout your life. His power is still the same. Day by day, as you continue to trust and receive God's healing power through learning the secret of meditating on scriptures every day and saying them aloud to make a spiritual deposit into your mind, soul, and spirit, this strategy will deliver you from mental health issues and premature deaths, you will not struggle with mental health issues or die prematurely. Instead, you will experience mental strength, mental restoration, and mental resilience for your wholeness and well-being holistically.

# CHAPTER 13

# THE POWER OF WORDS

Words can impact mental health, not just psychologically and spiritually. Words can heal or destroy a person as often as those words are used by the individual or against someone else. In today's world, some people don't take their abuse of words seriously, as mentioned in the Crisis & Trauma chapter. For example, there are common words that people label people ignorantly and maliciously for those who have suffered from mental illness. Words such as *crazy, mad, nutty, fruitcake, psycho, slow, retarded*, are hurtful words that society has allowed people to label those who suffer from mental illnesses, whether biologically or from a crisis. Mental illness is a severe pandemic that should never be stereotyped to dehumanize a person's humanity and dignity. Instead, mental illness should always be treated with care and compassion to help others who need healing.

Let's look at *words* from a spiritual standpoint. As mentioned in the previous chapter, God's Word and your words carry spiritual power. God used His Words to create the heavens, the world, and humanity. *Words* have sound, tone, vibration, and messages with definitions of the words that produce power to operate in one's life. Realize that words are a *spiritual language* that can influence your beliefs and mental health based on what you *read, meditate,* and constantly *hear.* Again, words are *spirit.* They can either wound or bring hope to someone. Proverbs 15:4 (MSG) says, "Kind words heal and help; cutting words wound and maim." Proverbs 18:21 (AMP) further explains this spiritual method: "Death and life are in the power of the tongue, And those who love it and indulge it will eat its fruit and bear the consequences of their words." So, God's Word in scripture, and His words spoken directly to you outside of scripture within your spirit, along with your spoken words, can cause things in your life to shift to the left or right. In other words, words can produce good or evil things to happen to you.

The beliefs, emotions, and attitude a person carries in their heart will affect their words. The next verse was mentioned in an earlier chapter but with additional instructions. Notably, it is, Proverbs 4:20-23 (NIV) says,

> My son, pay attention to what I say; turn your ear to my words. Do not let them out of your sight, keep them within your heart; for they are life to those who find them and health to one's whole body. Above all else, guard your heart, for everything you do flows from it.

See how these scriptures always attribute what you speak will control what happens in your life? Similarly, 1 Peter 3:10-13 (KJV) says,

> For he that would love life, and see good days, let him refrain his tongue from evil, and his lips that they speak no guile: Let him eschew evil, and do good; let him seek peace, and ensue it. For the eyes of the Lord are over the righteous, and his ears are open unto their prayers: but the face of the Lord is against them that do evil. And who is he that will harm you, if ye be followers of that which is good?

Here, God describes the secret to having a good life, is connected to a person's speech and daily words. So, not only should you be careful of your comments and be intentional about speaking positively about yourself but you should also be sure you don't put others down and verbally abuse them. Also, beware of people who are careless and violent with their mouths. In other words, they speak hurtful words and curse constantly to disrespect and demean others. This is verbal abuse. Negative remarks can break someone's spirit and kill their reputation, causing them a life of hardship and pain. Another powerful passage of truth to empower you to guard yourself from wicked people is Proverbs 18:1 (NIV) says, "An unfriendly person pursues selfish ends and against all sound judgment starts quarrels."

That is why it is essential for your mental health to never allow anyone to degrade you, dehumanize or devalue you because you are different from them or don't agree with them about something. Do not tolerate it at all. The first time it happens should be the last time you allow it. So remember to avoid relationships with people who curse all the time and always speak wickedly. They condemn their own lives and can tremendously curse yours if you tolerate this behavior. Not only should you be mindful of what you say about yourself, but also what others say about you and what you say about others. Love and respect yourself enough to protect your mental health and your entire life from destruction.

Therefore, discipline yourself to speak words that build you up from your mouth. Only gravitate to people who respectfully talk about the truth to you with grace, in a respectful manner that helps build you up. Guard your mind and spirit from pain and abuse. Instead, engage your spirit using words that bring life and peace to you.

## Prayer

Praying is also a powerful way to use words, speaking to God for amazing transformation, healing, and changes to happen in your life. Because prayer includes words that connect you with God from your human spirit to cause changes for the better in your life. Notably, answered prayers are not automatic. Sometimes God answers prayer because He is being merciful. However, for a person to experience complete healing and recovery from tragedies and problems in their lives, if there is unresolved sin in a person's life, they must walk away from sin. A person in prayer must, from the heart, repent of sin, surrender to God, receive His love and forgiveness, accept Jesus as Lord and Savior, receive God's Holy Spirit, begin to live by the spiritual principles of God, receive spiritual support from godly leaders, to disconnect from family and demonic curses and follow the directions of God for complete deliverance, healing, and victory of answered prayer to happen in one's life. As stated before, 1 Peter 3:10-13 (KJV) says,

> For he that would love life, and see good days, let him refrain his tongue from evil, and his lips that they speak no guile: Let him eschew evil, and do good; let him seek peace, and ensue it. For the eyes of the Lord are over the righteous, and his ears are open unto their prayers: but the face of the Lord is against them that do evil. And who is he that will harm you, if ye be followers of that which is good?

Understand, you must pray from your *human spirit* with words, not your mind. Compared to thoughts in your mind, your words will activate the dark world or the heavenly world of light from God for how your paths will be set and events happen in your life.

Similarly, James 5:16 (AMPC) says,

> Confess to one another therefore your faults (your slips, your false steps, your offenses, your sins) and pray [also] for one another, that you may be healed and restored [to a spiritual tone of mind and heart]. The earnest (heartfelt, continued) prayer of a righteous man makes tremendous power available [dynamic in its working].

So, not only should you pray to God as a form of reverence unto Him and to grow in relationship with Him, but also for His intervention during difficult times to help you get through them well. You also must learn to hear His voice and receive His guidance. Getting quiet and calm makes hearing and listening to God easier. That is why prayer is an essential power, using words that are scriptural to connect with God and making your requests for His guidance and help, and He will turn things around for the better for you in time if you wait on His timing and continue to keep your faith and trust in Him.

# CHAPTER 14

# THE POWER OF MUSIC

What is music? It is putting sounds together with words to express emotions. Regarding your mental health and spiritual wellness, some music can either uplift your mind and spirit or put you in a mood of depression. When it comes to music, many people focus on the artist or singer of the song and need to be more focused on the purpose and message of the music and song. Others pay attention to the melody and beat of a song more than the words. However, it is vital that you also listen carefully to the words of a song and its message and not just focus on the artist, the melody and move to the beat.

Music's *message*, *melody*, and *sound* can impact your mental health. For instance, music has the power to change your mood and mindset. Some studies show the impact of music relaxing your human spirit, uplifting your moods, and reducing stress. So, upbeat therapeutic songs can bring strength and comfort to your mind and spirit. For example, many Gospel songs uplift people from troubles, bringing them hope and encouragement that God will work everything out for them. Gospel music is therapeutic to your mind and spirit. Namely, a powerful known Gospel classic by *The Clark Sisters*, "You Brought The Sunshine." If you are having a rough day and are mentally overwhelmed, and your spirit feels down, pop this song on as it will uplift you. You can purchase some of these CDs at stores or online stores like Amazon; some may be available on Apple iTunes. King and Country is another powerful contemporary Christian/inspirational group and song, "God Only Knows."

**Here's a list of other uplifting songs for your mental health and spiritual wellness:**

Danny Gokey "Haven't Seen It Yet"
Hezekiah Walker "Jesus Is My Help"
Gary Oliver "He Really Will"
Carry Underwood "Jesus, Take The Will"
Toby Mac "All I Want Is You."
Chris Tomlin "And If Our God Is For Us"
The Newsboys "Your Love Never Fails"
Colton Dixon "Let Them See You"
Alan Jackson "What A Friend We Have In Jesus"

The melody from the instruments changes a person's mood from hopelessness to hope and from sadness to gladness about life. Also, the words bring cheer and connection to God of adoration, worship, strength, and comfort from the song's words. These songs will give you power and strength within you. As you listen to musical songs over and over and over again, your mind will memorize the words, and the song will become a part of how you think, feel, and act.

On the other hand, some music may bring gloom and darkness to your life. Some people call these songs the Blues or R&B Rhythm & Blues. The song or music intends to sympathize with the listener about one's pain or situation in life. This can be helpful to some people when processing their problems and hurt at first. However, a person need not remain in a state of feeling blue or the blues if they seek to get better. True, there is some positive R&B music that promotes healthy love and relationships, and there is a lot of upbeat music and songs that are not gospel songs that can inspire you and bring you happiness. Be sure they are clean and not immoral and do not disrespect God and humanity.

Another example is music and songs promoting satanic behavior and violence toward others. This can be dangerous to your mind, soul, and spirit. Because the words you *murmur* to yourself, *sing*, or *rap* subliminally may be satanic or unclean, which can negatively impact your thoughts, emotions, moods, and behaviors.

Therefore, be intentional about what music you listen to. Psalm 95:1-3 (KJV) says,

> O come, let us sing unto the Lord: let us make a joyful noise to the rock of our salvation. Let us come before his presence with thanksgiving, and make a joyful noise unto him with psalms. For the Lord is a great God, and a great King above all gods.

So be sure your music and songs have a positive, empowering message in the song that honors God and ministers to you, and uplift your spirit with strength and resilience.

# CHAPTER 15

# THE POWER OF WISDOM

Remember in a previous chapter how King Solomon in the Bible asked God for the gift of *wisdom*? After God granted King Solomon this gift, he became a legacy of *wisdom* and recorded many chapters on how to use wisdom in daily living. Wisdom is supernatural understanding from God with how to use knowledge in life. There is a powerful truth in the Bible from Proverbs 9:10 (KJV): "The fear of the Lord is the beginning of wisdom: and the knowledge of the holy is understanding." So, to reverence and honor your Creator is the beginning of you becoming a wise person.

There are levels of wisdom. The first one is the *spirit of wisdom.* This means being able to discern and understand people and situations and knowing how to use proper knowledge to resolve problems or improve things.

Then there is the *word of wisdom.* This level of insight allows a person to provide counsel or an answer to someone's dilemma or questions about a particular situation. This kind of wisdom provides answers and counsel about someone's future.

There are other benefits to receiving the *wisdom* of God. One area wisdom benefits you is understanding how to discern good and evil. King Solomon explains in the book of Proverbs the value of wisdom. Proverbs 4:5 (AMP) says, "Get [skillful and godly] wisdom! Acquire understanding [actively seek spiritual discernment, mature comprehension, and logical interpretation]! Do not forget nor turn away from the words of my mouth."

As you can see, *wisdom* empowers your thinking processes, judgment, and decision-making. Wisdom teaches you how to make wise choices at the right time. Notably, for conflict resolution, a wise person will choose the right time to speak with the right tone to address a problem and present a solution that prevents hurting others. Wisdom also gives you supernatural intelligence on how to relate to people of different cultures, races, and religions respectfully and clearly. Proverbs 15:1 (MSG) says, "A gentle response defuses anger, but a sharp tongue kindles a temper-fire."

Wisdom also gives you favor with God and people, not just in the church world but also in business. Walking in God's wisdom gives your character a good attitude and integrity with a wise perception about helping others become better people living a prosperous life through God.

Proverbs 4:8-9 (AMP) explains, Prize wisdom [and exalt her], and she will exalt you; She will honor you if you embrace her. She will place on your head a garland of grace; She will present you with a crown of beauty and glory.

Notably, wisdom from God that you receive from Him directly or through scripture will guide you into treasures of life, allowing others to see your noble character and help you succeed. Hence, wisdom from God allows you to develop meaningful relationships with others and brilliant strategies to make and maintain wealth with your health.

## COUNSELORS' WISDOM

It is wise and prudent also to seek the wisdom of others who have a close relationship with God, and the person also has good moral character and integrity and can healthily relate to others. Counsel for direction in life or problem-solving is also rewarding from a wise pastoral counselor, professional counselor, mentor, or friend. That is why Proverbs 11:14 (MSG) states, "Without good direction, people lose their way; the more wise counsel you follow, the better your chances." In the same way, Proverbs 11:14 (AMP) translation says, "Where there is no [wise, intelligent] guidance, the people fall [and go off course like a ship without a helm], But in the abundance of [wise and godly] counselors there is victory." Therefore, seeking counsel is wise and can protect you from needless pain and unnecessary mistakes and issues in life. Receiving counsel from those who have experienced mistakes in life and also have the education to guide you into truth and safety will empower your mental health and spiritual wellness. As a result, wise counsel will preserve your life.

## A Proverb A Day

As you can see, wisdom from God makes things easier in life. Wisdom teaches you how to resolve problems in your life. So, if you fear the Lord, you have already stepped into receiving the gift of wisdom. Allowing suitable counselors in your life makes you even wiser. Now, you have to allow wisdom to grow in your life. Therefore, to continue empowering your mind and spirit to think right and make smart decisions, reading a *Proverb* once or thrice a day will do wonders for your mental and spiritual health.

# CHAPTER 16

# RESHAPING THE SOUL

Did you know your soul was created by God to live forever? Depending upon how a person lives, their *soul* will either live with God in peace forever or with the devil in torment forever. That is why scripture says from Mark 8:36-37 (KJV), "For what shall it profit a man, if he shall gain the whole world, and lose his own soul? Or what shall a man give in exchange for his soul?" This scripture is an important message for all humanity to think sincerely about how one lives and cares for their soul. Notably, your soul is the core of your identity, carrying your thoughts, desires, feelings, emotions, and memories.

In the cases of surviving crisis and trauma, your *soul* is one of the most vital parts of you that will need the most work for healing. After your soul has battled, endured, and processed the pain and suffering of crises and trauma, your soul needs recovery and reshaping. This process will begin with changing your perspective about how you deal with yourself and the recovery process, changing your thought processes, learning coping and stress management skills, and spiritual methods towards the reshaping and renewing your *soul*.

Knowing yourself and understanding where you are, psychologically and emotionally, after a crisis is vital to your recovery and reshaping your soul. So during this process, you must take time to rediscover yourself by knowing your strengths, weaknesses, and limitations, then rebuild the new you by committing to yourself rebuilding your life through a healing process. Because the condition of your soul will either build or break down your human spirit and character. 3 John 2:2 (KJV) says, "Beloved, I wish above all things that thou mayest prosper and be in health, even as thy soul prospereth." Here, God is emphasizing the importance of being healthy in every area of your life, which includes avoiding living a broken and destructive life. That is why you must reshape your soul by guarding it against corrupt beliefs against God, unclean images, negative words, and wicked people.

One of the steps to reshaping your soul is to be mindful of what you expose your eyes and ears to. In other words, do not invite terror and unclean television and radio programming or negative music to your eyes and ears, or it will attach to your soul, fill your mind with negative thought patterns, and corrupt it. Don't let the devil, society, social media, and the world control your soul. Choose carefully how to care for and deposit what goes into your soul that will nourish and build up your mind, will, and emotions. That is why the Bible says from Proverbs 4:23 (CSB) says, "Guard your heart above all else, for it is the source of life." Proverbs 4:23 (AMP) translation says, "Watch over your heart with all diligence, For from it flow the springs of life." God's will for you is to enjoy life, but first, you must get a handle on your soul.

Be careful also about where you spend your time. Don't hang around atheists who don't respect God, and live immoral lives. 1 Corinthians 15:33 (KJV) says, "Be not deceived: evil communications corrupt good manners." This means that being in the wrong environment or hanging around wicked people too long will influence you to conform to their thinking and ways. Because your spirit and soul become whatever it continues to be exposed to. It is a spiritual law. Whatever you invest most of your time will influence how you think, feel, and act. So do not spend time in wicked places around negative, immoral people. Also, do not corrupt your eyes and ears by watching immoral activities through a demonic event, a movie, harmful television shows, radio, or corrupt and unclean reading materials that promote wickedness. Do not corrupt your soul and spirit with immorality. Mark 8:36 (KJV) says, "For what shall it profit a man, if he shall gain the whole world, and lose his own soul?" Your soul is more important than the world's views of power, prestige, and material wealth.

On the contrary, Luke 21:19 (KJV) says, "In your patience possess ye your souls." Luke 21:19 (AMP) says, "By your [patient] endurance [empowered by the Holy Spirit] you will gain your souls." So, when you decide to put away an immoral lifestyle and submit to God's way of living through Jesus in purity and righteousness, you will have possession of your soul and a peaceful soul. When you can control your soul, you can manage your life.

So don't fill your eyes, ears, and time invested in corrupt living. Instead, fill your eyes and ears with good things. For example, if you are in a hostile environment, leave that place as soon as possible. Find a new environment that is clean and positive, and surround yourself with positive people who think like you and with positive pursuits in life. This helps safeguard your soul from crises and conditions your soul for healing. Also, build your soul with the correct beliefs, spiritual knowledge, words, and mental health strategies. Disciplining yourself to read and listen to wholesome teachings promoting a pure life in God and healthy living is a vital part of this process. Not only will you purify your soul from darkness, wickedness, and sickness, but you will also strengthen your mind, will, and emotions to walk in purity and healthiness, giving you energy, and motivation, and wellness through God empowering your life. No matter what life throws at you, your soul will be fortified and shaped to make it through any trial with personal growth and comfort because God is with you.

## The Five P's of the Resilience Umbrella

The resilience umbrella is a healthy guide mentioned in my other book as the Author titled, *Untraumatized*. The resilience umbrella is explained as the process of normal human functioning that not only helps in reshaping your soul but also prepares your soul to accept the reality of any event that happened to you and, when it is a crisis, to be prepared with <u>biblical knowledge</u>, <u>spiritual principles,</u> and <u>mental health strategies,</u> and develop grit to adapt and adjust from shock, distress, and mental injury, to normalcy and recovery. There are *five stages* to the resiliency process. This is a professional guideline for healing and recovery from crisis and trauma or resolving other life challenges.

**Paradigms.** Changing your thought processes and patterns about improving one's life is the first step. In other words, before and after a crisis, being hopeful instead of hopeless begins the path of healing and recovery from tragedies. Being mindful of the beliefs you live by determines your perspectives of your healing path. Studying your reactions during challenging times and focusing on solutions promotes healing. God's Word in the Bible is the best way you can train your mind to have biblical meditations, beliefs, and words to live by, which will transform your attitude, heal your emotions, improve your self-image, and give you a brighter perspective and motivation about how to process adversities in your life with adaptability and strength to move forward in life with positive goals and purpose.

**Principles.** There are fundamental truths that will help you recover from anxiety, terror, hurt, pain, and loss a person suffers after a crisis. For example, applying biblical principles of meditation scriptures of God's healing, redemptive power, and protection from Psalm 23 contributes to regulating your emotions to hope, peace, and restoration, which is soul healing. Another example is using mental health techniques to maintain mental wellness, such as abstaining and avoiding oneself from drugs and alcoholism. Keeping up with eating healthy foods and drinking lots of water contributes to your physical health, which promotes your mental wellness. Abiding by these beliefs helps you discipline your behaviors and protect your soul from unnecessary pain. As a result, your soul is being protected from darkness, *pain, bruises,* and *wounds,* but instead, your soul is being nourished by God's Words and mental health techniques to relieve stress and build inner strength to adapt and adjust to life's challenges. This process empowers you with grit and resilience.

*Pause.* Pausing is also a critical learning step when overcoming a past crisis and trauma. Training yourself to get quiet and calm when tragedy strikes is a helpful decision to protect yourself from becoming overwhelmed by a nervous breakdown. *Counting to ten* is a way to help calm your nerves to a state of relaxation and self-control. This kind of pausing gives you time to think of a plan to get to a place of safety and get help. Pausing also allows your soul to rest, revive, and recover from the distress of a crisis. James 1:19-21 (AMP) also teaches and empowers you to control your spirit, regulate your emotions and temperament, and be wise with your speech by stating,

> Understand this, my beloved brothers and sisters. Let everyone be quick to hear [be a careful, thoughtful listener], slow to speak [a speaker of carefully chosen words and], slow to anger [patient, reflective, forgiving]; for the resentful, deep-seated] anger of man does not produce the righteousness of God [that standard of behavior which He requires from us]. So get rid of all uncleanness and all that remains of wickedness, and with a humble spirit receive the word [of God] which is implanted [actually rooted in your heart], which is able to save your souls.

As you can see, following these steps cleanses, nourishes, and reshapes your soul to healing.

*Prayer.* Being prayerful is another vital stage of healing and recovery of the soul. After experiencing a catastrophe, some people may suffer distress, mental illness, demonic oppression, and are tempted to sin. However, prayers to God will bring a person help, comfort, and recovery provisions. As stated before, answered prayers are not automatic. Again, for a person to experience complete healing and recovery from tragedies and problems in their lives, if there is unresolved sin in a person's life, they must walk away from sin. A person in prayer must, from the heart, surrender to God, repent of sin, receive His love and forgiveness, accept Jesus as Lord and Savior, receive God's Holy Spirit, begin to live by the spiritual principles of God, receive spiritual support from godly leaders, to disconnect from family and demonic curses and follow the directions of God for complete deliverance, healing, and victory of answered prayer to happen in one's life. Through this process, God's grace will be with those who sincerely seek His truth, help, cleansing, and redemption. As stated earlier in a previous chapter, there are scriptural prayers you can pray to help you become well with God's help. Psalm 73:26 (KJV) says, "My flesh and my heart faileth: but God is the strength of my heart, and my portion for ever." Psalm 119:28 (KJV) also says, "My soul melteth for heaviness: strengthen thou me according unto thy word." Similarly, Psalm 119:28 (AMP) says, "My soul dissolves because of grief; Renew and strengthen me according to [the promises of] Your word." Here, your soul refers to (your mind, will, and emotions), that God wants to heal. Additionally, to get spiritual support from the church for healing and recovery, James 5:13-15 (MSG) says,

Are you hurting? Pray. Do you feel great? Sing. Are you sick? Call the church leaders together to pray and anoint you with oil in the name of the Master. Believing-prayer will heal you, and Jesus will put you on your feet. And if you've sinned, you'll be forgiven, healed inside and out.

***Personal growth.*** Personal growth is the result of managing the other *4 Ps of resilience*. As you use all *four* stages of resilience to prepare for a crisis or after a crisis, your soul is being reshaped and restored to wellness, which is personal growth. Afterward, you will begin to experience self-development, in which you will begin to recognize that you have developed the inner strength and stamina to bear through, adapt, and adjust during and after crises without falling apart. But instead, you bounce back from the crisis and continue functioning without depression and wanting to resort to sin or substance abuse. Relying on God is critical to your personal growth. Knowing your limitations and strengths is essential for personal development and spiritual growth. Notably, Psalm 138:3 (KJV) says, "In the day when I cried thou answeredst me, and strengthenedst me with strength in my soul." So, by staying prayerful to God and asking for His grace (favor and the capacity to handle life's pressures), He will strengthen you and sustain you through hard times. So, don't try to be so much in control of your life without God's help. Remember, you need His spiritual power through prayer to be strengthened and comforted, with the ability to resist falling into darkness. James 4:7 (KJV) says, "Submit yourselves therefore to God. Resist the devil, and he will flee from you." So as you follow God's Word, and surrender to His ways, the devil and wicked powers will not have control over you. Instead of being taken over by trials in your life, God will empower you to overcome storms while you keep a positive attitude about life, depending on God for strength and comfort.

## Self-Care

You owe it to yourself to love yourself, be good to yourself, and take care of yourself. Protect yourself, and avoid people, places, and things, that cause you mental harm and spiritual abuse. Good hygiene is also vital to your human spirit, mental health, and physical body.

*Hydrotherapy.* This kind of water therapy has been an ancient method many asylums and mental hospitals used to help cure their patients. Here, the water awakens those in mental distress and is a form of cleansing. Notably, cleanliness removes mental illness.

Moreover, from a spiritual perspective, water baptism is a sacred activity Christians participate in to experience a greater connection with God and sign of washing away the old life while entering into a new life in Jesus through water baptism. Furthermore, in the Bible, Ezekiel 36:25-27 (NIV) says from God,

I will sprinkle clean water on you, and you will be clean; I will cleanse you from all your impurities and from all your idols. I will give you a new heart and put a new spirit in you; I will remove from you your heart of stone and give you a heart of flesh. And I will put my Spirit in you and move you to follow my decrees and be careful to keep my laws.

Wow! Do you see how water can spiritually and physically carry a spiritual power to wash away sin and mental bondage? Likewise, this is why some mental hospitals used hydrotherapy to help diminish mental illness conditions in their patients. Today, people can use this own form of therapy in their homes as therapy with scheduled showers or baths using clean water spiritually and physically wash away the dirt from their lives to refresh their human spirit and mind from dark emotions and gloom to newness and restoration of their soul, spirit, and body for healing and recovery of themselves.

Changing your environment is also vital to the process of reshaping your soul. The neighborhood and condition of a house you reside in affect your thought processes, behaviors, and human functioning. Living in a safe neighborhood, in a decent home that is elegant, clean, organized, and spacious, is a healthy environment promoting spiritual health and mental wellness. When a habitat and home are clean and not a hot spot for crimes, your soul will not continue to struggle with anxiety, fear, and distress. Instead, your soul can experience a life of tranquility and peace.

***Facial Care.*** Do you value the unique image and reflection of yourself in the mirror? One of the first images you see is your face. How you see yourself, which is your self-image is vital to your self-acceptance and self-worth. You might have had diminishing thoughts about the size of your eyes, nose, or eyebrows. However, God made you just the way He wanted you to look. Don't devalue any part of your face.

Appreciate the artwork God designed to create you. Your face is how you connect with your inner self and show up among others. Therefore, you must take good care of your face and your teeth. Keep your face clean with soap and water daily. Notably, use the right soap and skin products suitable for you to keep your skin looking healthy.

If you are a woman, keep your skin clean and appreciate your natural beauty before adding makeup. It is every woman's individual choice as to whether or not she wants to wear makeup. No one should judge a woman's preference for makeup. However, your intentions and motives should always be pure and not for harmful purposes. Modesty is essential to embracing your natural beauty while enhancing your face. Choosing the right color tones and shades when wearing makeup goes a long way in enhancing your beauty. This promotes a healthy self-image.

For men, keeping your face clean and healthy is also important. It is your decision whether you choose to wear facial hair. If so, proper grooming of your facial hair regularly helps secure your identity and promotes a healthy self-image.

*Hair Care.* Taking care of your hair is essential for your mental health. If you are a woman, visits to the beauty parlor are a good way to relax, get a good scalp massage, a good washing, conditioning, and hair styling will do wonders for your mental health.

Likewise, men who groom their hairstyles and faces, or go to barber shops for proper hair care, help them to feel refreshed, and help their minds feel better. Anyone who keeps up with styling their hair will help provide a sense of peace to their minds. Hair care also boosts your self-esteem and self-image to feel good about yourself. You deserve it! It is essential to make time for yourself for restoration, for your health and well-being to live a balanced life.

According to (Lewis, 2022, p. 130), here are some other helpful self-care techniques to help you decompress and reshape your soul to promote mental health and spiritual wellness for a balanced life:

1. A Positive, Safe Environment
2. A Hot Shower or Bath
3. Prayer and Reading Devotionals with God
4. Healthy Nutrition
5. Christian/Inspirational Music
6. Making a Vision Board
7. New Positive Hobbies
8. Daily Walks
9. Exercising
10. Visiting Family and Friends
11. Road Trips
12. Attending Christian-Based Church, Counseling, Group Therapy, and Mental Health Support Groups
13. Drinking Tea or Coffee

14. Journaling feelings, special events, and accomplishing positive goals.
15. Sleep and Rest

## Put Total Trust in No one

As you continue to experience self-development and the refreshing and renewing of your soul, you must learn a fundamental truth about humanity. If you want to maintain your inner peace and prevent becoming brokenhearted repeatedly, never put your total trust in anyone because people are not perfect and can fail you unintentionally and intentionally. This refers to a spouse, child, relative, friends, clergy, colleagues, counselors, and strangers.

Although there are people that care about you and love you, you are to treasure that and can have a certain level of trust and confidence in them, but never trust them to a point where you don't believe they are capable of not having wrong beliefs about something, wrong you, or make a mistake. Notably, this is critical to understand in the church world and avoid being *church hurt*. People are human and cannot be everything to everyone. Some people's problems will cause them to flip on you and be ill toward you.

People can also be moody and change their ideas, beliefs, and feelings about things in life. This can be shocking and hurtful if you don't guard your heart and soul from becoming too dependent on people. That is why in the Bible, God said through Jeremiah 17:5-7 (NLT) says,

This is what the Lord says: Cursed are those who put their trust in mere humans, who rely on human strength and turn their hearts away from the Lord. They are like stunted shrubs in the desert, with no hope for the future. They will live in the barren wilderness, in an uninhabited salty land. But blessed are those who trust in the Lord and have made the Lord their hope and confidence.

As you can see, God is trying to protect your soul from disappointment and hurt because human beings can fail you because of their faulty beliefs and challenging circumstances. Sometimes it's not always a matter of right or wrong. It is just that people can change and not live up to your expectations because of their issues.

In other cases, people want to help you but cannot because of their limitations. But God will never fail you. He may not always give you what you want, but it is for the best. He created you and knows the beginning to the end, so trust that God is taking care of your life. So, if you don't worship people and expect too much, it won't break your spirit if they let you down. Understanding this reality is especially critical in the church world to avoid church hurt. Again, God is your Creator and should be Who you put your total trust in because He made you and knows what is best for you!

So when others fail you, you don't have to feel bad about yourself and allow it to ruin your day or be like them. You can also strive to be better and be a kind person of integrity to the best of your ability with God's help. When others fail you or become mean or untrustworthy, you don't have to become like these people. You can always guard your heart from shady people while building healthy relationships with others in your family, church, workplace, friends, and counselors. Because those who have your best interest at heart will do their best to be good to you in a relationship with you, and when they make an error, they will apologize and fix it to maintain a healthy relationship.

Understanding about how far to trust humanity will help you keep your mental wellness. You will not be surprised if people fail you. But you can also cherish the people who continue to respect you and be well toward you. Keep those people close to you. Believe and have some confidence in people based on their moral character, but only put your total trust in God and live for Him. As a result, it will be well with your soul.

## Laughter

Did you realize that smiling or even laughing can help heal your soul? The Bible Proverbs 17:22 (KJV) says, "A merry heart doeth good like a medicine: but a broken spirit drieth the bones." Here, a happy heart strengthens your spirit, and builds resilience in you to face life each new day with hope and a positive attitude. Notably, comedy should not disrespect God or other's dignity or promote immorality. However, clean comedy is a healing agent that transforms a broken heart into a glad heart.

## The Fight In You

Keep a fight in you! Don't ever give up on yourself, no matter how difficult things get. It would help if you remembered you have endured so much and made it through this far. When it seems too difficult, remember it is always helpful to call for support, encouragement, guidance, and prayer, whether a spouse, friend, godly leader, or professional counselor. This is you fighting for your life, the fight in you that promotes maintaining your mental health.

*Post-Traumatic Growth.* Comparatively, *post-traumatic growth* works simultaneously with personal development. In psychology, this concept is explained as having the ability to adapt to normalcy and understand oneself after a traumatic experience. As you can see, post-traumatic growth strengthens your soul to bear through crises and recover with grit, courage, hope, energy, a positive attitude, and strength. Post-Traumatic growth shows you where you have grown as a person. What used to bother you will not bother you as much anymore. Journaling helps you to identify your thoughts, emotions, and feelings and allows you to reflect on your self-development. After you get back up after a tragedy in your life, always be intentional about planning healthy goals to pursue toward your wellness. It will provide independence and meaningful purpose in your life and post-traumatic growth and resilience.

# CHAPTER 17

# SPIRITUAL CARE & MORE

Spiritual care is vital for your continued mental health and spiritual wellness. So for continued spiritual care, seek counsel from a counselor who models a moral lifestyle unto God. Counselors such as pastors and Christian counselors from agencies can help you work through spiritual problems and provide solutions to help you resolve them. However, counselors should first learn your beliefs and values as a client regarding God and His Word in your life. As a client, you must be willing to discuss your spiritual problems and sins with the counselor if trust has already been established. Ethical boundaries are also essential for building a professional relationship between counselor and client.

Spiritual or pastoral care in counseling is also necessary to blend with psychology, mental healthcare, and theology. In other words, there are elements of integrating psychology, theology, and spirituality in counseling. One of the first elements is having the foundation of knowledge and understanding of how all three work individually and can be intertwined in your counseling as a client from a holistic perspective. This is a way theologians can understand the science of psychology and clients' cognitive and behavioral patterns and learn how to connect God's Word and His spiritual power with their client's healing process. The other element is the importance of blending Christian spirituality into counseling to help hurting clients realize their need for God as one of the core healing methods through a relationship with Him. Because God's primary purpose for humanity was to love Him, themselves, and others spiritually and relationally.

Scriptures in Christian counseling and psychotherapy can be blended models that help clients connect with God and help change their mindset, behaviors, and emotions. The counseling experience allows transformation of oneself to take place as a result of using Bible scriptures as a foundational technique in counseling to help bring healing to clients. Counselors are in a position to foster hope in clients who feel worthless. Attending counseling for clients can produce hope as a redemptive way to get their lives back in order and find some peace. The client can be won over to salvation in Jesus Christ by the kindness, wisdom, truth, and support they receive from their counselors.

So this means counselors who share theology and teach clients about God's love, prayer, and the importance of meditating on scripture can motivate them to apply these spiritual practices, which are effective for them to get better in all areas of their lives. Namely, how clients think, feel, and respond differently to challenges in their lives through encounters with God and learning that He will uplift them through any challenge will produce healing and build resilience in clients. So, keeping God in the center of your life will holistically allow you to continue a life of well-being, home life, career, community work, and building and maintaining healthy relationships with others.

Pastoral or Christian counselors will also highlight prayer as a vital discipline to aid a client's mental and spiritual wellness. It is how a client connects with God, humanity's source of life and strength. Once the counselor has been able to help guide you as the client to the spiritual source of strength and transformation through Jesus Christ, change and resilience can begin developing in the client, and the scriptures can continue to be the foundation of one's view of self and trust in God. Through this process, your spirit, soul, and body should unite in unison to help the other function holistically. Integrating biblical knowledge and psychology is a helpful counseling intervention technique for a client's spiritual and emotional health, validation, self-worth, identity, and self-image.

## Human Services

Through community agencies, Human Services provides mental health advocacy and counseling roles to help the public, such as family and grief counseling, case management, and life skills instructions. Human service workers provide government and community resources instead of their own money to help clients needing human service care medically, emotionally, or for housing needs. These services can help the client regain stability, independence, and wellness in their lives.

## Professional Counseling

If you are struggling with trauma from a previous crisis or mental health issues, get help, and seek professional counseling, starting with scheduling a consultation through a referral or seeking help on your own. This is essential for your mental health and well-being. Getting help doesn't make you weak. It makes you well.

Different types of mental health professionals have other treatment methods for mental illnesses and personal crises. Each of these professionals connects with the clients through a healthy rapport and discussion to identify their issues and provide solutions to support clients' healing. A vital resource used to help assess clients' needs is the Diagnostic Statistic Manual (DSM). This manual book helps mental health professionals diagnose the symptoms and descriptions of mental illnesses. During the assessment stage, mental health professionals first want to ensure a safe environment for the clients to discuss their mental health needs.

One of the mental health professionals is a *psychiatrist*. Notably, they can diagnose mental health disorders with behavioral and emotional problems. Psychotherapy and prescribing medications are their primary treatment plans for clients.

*Psychologists* focus on the psychological state of a client. They also help clients identify their thinking and behavioral patterns. Afterward, they provide solution-focused counseling to help clients identify their issues, process their pain, regulate their emotions, and experience personal growth.

Similarly, professional counselors provide mental health counseling to help heal those with mental health issues and provide coping skills for stress management. But first, a consent form and the terms of counseling sessions are established. In the first counseling session, counselors establish trust and emotional connection while determining treatment options. Counselors can also evaluate how the trauma attacks affected their clients by allowing them to share their stories or illustrate their feelings on paper. Counselors can help clients identify their weaknesses and highlight their strengths to work through their psychological issues to heal successfully.

One of the most common mental disorders people struggle with from chronic problems in their life or after crises is a disorder called General Anxiety Disorder (GAD). Clinically, a standard mental health treatment for dealing with anxiety issues and other mental health disorders is called Cognitive Behavioral Therapy (CBT). Notably, cognitive behavioral therapy allows counselors to help their clients identify their stressors and emotional issues, and they talk through how to find coping techniques and problem-solving skills to reduce or eliminate stress.

Cognitive Behavioral Therapy (CBT) provides exposure therapy of something the client fears or is stressed about for coping skills. Whether it be exposure through imagery or memory of a traumatic event during therapy, the counselor aids the client in talking through the fear for healing. Facing the fear or issue repeatedly can help the client practice coping with the dread they feel in a healthy way until they are not negatively affected by a traumatic memory or image.

Self-compassion is a therapeutic technique counselors can offer to teach clients during their healing process, whether during home visits or office visits. A counselor showing a client how to help heal oneself, starting with letting go of self-pity and self-hate, and valuing oneself, is a part of this process. In other words, counselors provide helpful strategies, share coping skills, and collaborate with clients to formulate a plan for healthy pursuit and goals to support their healing needs. These techniques will help the client develop a sense of themselves and learn to love and value themselves beyond the trauma.

## Group Counseling

Another counseling intervention is offering group counseling support and mental health care for survivors of crisis and trauma. Sometimes the client has already established individual counseling with a professional counselor, who often refers them to group counseling for additional support. Group support allows you not to feel alone and understood during hardships in life. You can also gather some helpful knowledge on working through life's challenges from others in the support group.

### Counseling Referrals

The National Alliance for Mental Illness is a helpful resource for receiving support for mental health education. This organization also provides counseling support and other community resources for psychological and physical wellness. Individuals and their families can receive the counseling and education needed to promote mental health and healing in their lives. Here is the website, https://nami.org/Support-Education/Mental-Health-Education/NAMI-Hearts-Minds.

The National Suicide Prevention Line is another organization to support those struggling with depression and suicidal thoughts. If you feel hopeless and like ending your life, don't! A crisis phone line is available to call for emergencies. Do not procrastinate, and do not be ashamed. Get the help you need and call 1-800-273-8255. You owe to yourself or anyone who needs help not dying by suicide to save your life. You matter, and so does your life.

The National Domestic Violence Hotline is also a great support system for getting out of an abusive relationship. Their phone number is 1-800-799-7233. The representatives can guide you with counseling support and resources to get to a safe place, begin rebuilding your life, and receive your healing.

Another helpful resource that supports adults and children recovering from broken families is called Divorcecare. The website information is https://www.divorcecare.org/. It is a worldwide service that selects churches to offer throughout the United States. It provides support groups for parents and a separate one for children to recover from the pain of family disruption from marital break-ups. This support group is offered through registration online and is available near the end and beginning of each calendar year. Since families and broken couples struggle with memories and adjusting to being single and raising children alone, as well as children working through the transition of limited time with the parent outside of the home, this agency helps bring hope and suggestions to work through the pain and find happiness through this period.

## EDUCATION & PROFESSIONAL ASSOCIATIONS

Taking courses on mental health or crisis and trauma-informed training to earn credits and certifications can be beneficial in promoting your mental wellness. Some people decide to go to college to become professionals in the mental health field, which can also be helpful for their knowledge and well-being. There are also professional organizations that community wellness agencies, hospitals, and crisis intervention organizations you can look into from your community for mental health education and support.

## Healing Cycles

Realize anyone, no matter what age, who has experienced crisis and trauma will go through healing cycles through their recovery process. In other words, people process crisis and trauma differently, with different timetables for healing.

It may be a matter of months or a new milestone of healing when a new year approaches in one's life. Suppose spiritual care and mental health support are provided right away. In that case, the healing process will likely progress healthily, and the survivor will not suffer as long as someone who prolongs getting professional help for their healing and recovery.

So it is essential to recognize acute stress, anxiety, depression, and grief symptoms to get the spiritual care and professional care needed for healing and recovery. The Bible says, "Where no counsel is, the people fall: but in the multitude of counsellors there is safety" (Proverbs 11:14, KJV). So, Biblical and psychological intervention methods for survivors of crisis and trauma are an essential part of clients' holistic healing, emotionally and physically, which can benefit them spiritually. After all, God says, "Beloved, I wish above all things that thou mayest prosper and be in health, even as thou soul prospereth" (3 John 2:2, KJV).

Therefore, integrating biblical knowledge and psychology is always a helpful counseling intervention technique for counseling or therapy for a client's spiritual and emotional health, validation, self-worth, identity, and self-image. If a person has been through crisis and trauma, assessment, professional care, and spiritual care are needed for mental health, emotional regulation, healing, and suicide prevention. Helping survivors collaborate with new goals to pursue in their wellness will provide independence and meaningful purpose in one's life and post-traumatic growth and resilience.

In summary, remember, it is God's perfect will for you to be well, spirit, soul, and body holistically. Being whole in your spirit, soul, and body, is living a well balanced life. Acts 17:28 (KJV) apostle Paul said about God, "For in him we live, and move, and have our being; as certain also of your own poets have said, For we are also his offspring." In other words, without God's power, humanity would not exist. He is life, and His Word is always life-giving and helps you thrive in life.

Also, when it comes to the seasons of life experiences and the ups and downs of trials and blessings humanity faces, keep in mind Ecclesiastes 3:1-8 (KJV), which says,

To every thing there is a season, and a time to every purpose under the heaven: A time to be born, and a time to die; a time to plant, and a time to pluck up that which is planted; A time to kill, and a time to heal; a time to break down, and a time to build up; A time to weep, and a time to laugh; a time to mourn, and a time to dance; A time to cast away stones, and a time to gather stones together; a time to embrace, and a time to refrain from embracing; A time to get, and a time to lose; a time to keep, and a time to cast away; A time to rend, and a time to sew; a time to keep silence, and a time to speak; A time to love, and a time to hate; a time of war, and a time of peace."

God is never celebrating evil or promoting it. On the contrary, in this poetic prophecy about the seasons of life, God is helping you to understand the right purpose and timing of why things happen and how He wants humanity to navigate through life with their hope and trust in Him. It also explains God's kingdom, His justice for reproving evil, paths to walk, and His prophetic ways and blessings for all of humanity. Again, this powerful passage of scriptures will help you navigate the seasons of life. It is God's message of encouragement and resilience to fortify, strengthen, and comfort you through every season of life.

So remember, God is the foundation of all healing and wellness. But He also uses other resources such as spiritual leaders, professional counselors, medical professionals, medications, healthy food and drink consumption, and family and friend support to help us through life's adversities. Remember, when times are difficult, reflect on Isaiah 43:2 (KJV) scripture says, "When thou passest through the waters, I will be with thee; and through the rivers, they shall not overflow thee: when thou walkest through the fire, thou shalt not be burned; neither shall the flame kindle upon thee." In other words, God is your source of life, strength, and power to help you overcome any obstacle and hurt. So continue to open your heart to Him through Jesus Christ and be filled with His Holy Spirit to experience intimacy in God and His healing and goodness in your life through eternity.

# Mental Health Checkup

*Are you okay today?*

**Here is a checklist you should ask yourself daily for your mental health wellness:**

What's on your mind today?

Is there anything in your soul troubling you?

Did you or someone else cause you any hurt?

What emotion are you feeling at this time?

Did you have prayer with God and devotional time?

Have you taken care of your hygiene?

Did you eat a healthy meal and drink a healthy drink today?

Have you tried some of the power foods for alertness and strength today?

Is there someone you feel safe talking to as a friend, mentor, or professional counselor?

What helpful solutions have worked before to help resolve any problems in your life?

# REFERENCES

Evans, D. (Director). (2018). *Indivisible* [Film]. IMDb

https://nami.org/Support-Education/Mental-Health-Education/
NAMI-Hearts-Minds

https://www.acf.hhs.gov/fysb/programs/family-violence-prevention-
services/programs/ndvh

https://www.biblegateway.com

https://www.divorcecare.org/

*King James Bible*. (2004). Publisher: Thomas Nelson. (Original work
published 1798)

Lewis, Dr. S. (2022). *Untraumatized.* Pennsauken, NJ: Bookbaby